322
Machine
Knitting
Stitches

Sterling Publishing Co., Inc.   New York

Library of Congress Cataloging-in-Publication Data

Harmony guide to machine knitting stitches.   Volume 1.
    322 machine knitting stitches.
        p.   cm.
    Originally published: The Harmony guide to machine knitting
stitches. v. 1. Great Britain : Lyric Books, © 1988.
    ISBN 0-8069-8466-X
    1. Knitting, Machine—Patterns.   I. Title.   II. Title: Three
hundred twenty-two machine knitting stitches.
TT680.H354   1991
746.9'2—dc20   91–13264
                                                                 CIP

Compiled by Barbara Devaney

10 9 8 7 6 5 4 3 2 1

Published in North America in 1991 by
Sterling Publishing Company, Inc.
387 Park Avenue South, New York, N.Y. 10016
Originally published in Great Britain under the
title *The Harmony Guide to Machine Knitting Stitches:
Volume One* © 1988 by Lyric Books Limited
Distributed in Canada by Sterling Publishing
% Canadian Manda Group, P.O. Box 920, Station U
Toronto, Ontario, Canada M8Z 5P9
Printed and bound in Belgium
All rights reserved

Sterling ISBN 0-8069-8466-X

CONTENTS

Introduction

Machine knitting is a fascinating craft enabling knitted fabrics to be produced much more quickly than when knitted by hand. The variety of stitches which can be made is almost unlimited and there are very few effects occurring in hand knitting that cannot be produced by machine. However, the knitting machine should not just be looked on as an extension of hand knitting — there are many effects which can be easily produced on a machine which would not be worth doing by hand!

Machines

All knitting machines have a bed of needles which produce stocking stitch and an infinite variety of stocking stitch variations. Many machines nowadays have facilities that enable them to produce patterns automatically. The diagrams on the following pages have been designed with the most common method of automatic patterning — the 24 stitch punchcard — in mind. It is possible to reproduce most of the patterns indicated in this way manually if you do not have a punchcard machine and detailed explanations are given at the beginning of each chapter to enable you to translate the punchcard illustration into instructions for your machine.

Gauge

Most 24 stitch punchcard machines are standard gauge. They work best using 4 ply yarn but will also knit finer and some slightly thicker yarns. The samples shown have been knitted using 4 ply wool yarn on a standard gauge machine. A different effect can be achieved by using a chunky gauge machine with large needles and thicker yarn.

Yarn

It is very important to prepare yarn before knitting. Irregular stitches can result from yarn that has not been adequately prepared. Ideally it should be wound onto a cone or into a ball using a mechanical ball winder. A commercially wound ball of yarn can be used so long as the end is taken from the centre and it is placed in a jar or box to prevent it rolling around.

The more hairy yarns should also be waxed to enable the knit carriage to run freely. Paraffin wax, available from machine stockists or a candle can be held against the yarn whilst it is being wound.

Alternatively some machines have a place to hold wax so that the yarn comes into contact with it before passing to the knit carriage. Any wax remaining on the finished knitted fabric can be removed with the first wash.

Most standard knitting machines work best when using a smooth, fine yarn. The chunky machines can handle a wider variety of yarn. With care it is possible to knit more hairy or looped yarns of the correct thickness even on standard gauge machines. However, care must be taken when using such yarns that they do not catch on the gate posts. To check for caught loops run your fingers across the back of the knitting. A gentle downward tug of the work should release them. The more obstinate ones can be released using a latch tool. Do not be discouraged from using the more fancy yarns as they can give added interest to fabrics. For instance, try using a hairy or looped yarn as the contrast colour in a 2 colour fairisle.

Tension

It is essential when knitting a garment either from a commercial design or a design of your own to check your tension. This is done by knitting tension swatches in the yarn or yarns to be used for the garment.

To check each pattern tension cast on about 30 stitches and knit about 20 cms [8 ins] (refer to your machine handbook for suggested tension dial number). The knitting must then be allowed to relax completely, as the stitches have been stretched out while on the machine. If the yarn used is a wool or wool/synthetic mixture it will help the yarn to relax if steamed thoroughly without allowing the weight of the iron to rest on the work. If the yarn is predominantly synthetic ease the work in with your fingers and allow it to rest for as long as possible.

If you are working from a commercial design, mark with pins the number of stitches and rows as stated in the instructions to give 10 cms [4 ins] square, or the measurement stated. If this does not measure exactly the stated measurement, work another tension piece tighter (if the piece is too large) or looser (if the piece is too small). Continue in this way until you find the correct tension.

If you are going to use a punchcard pattern sample to design a garment of your own, continue testing until you have a sample that is at a suitable tension.

This may seem to be a long, complicated procedure but with time it should become automatic. Care taken at this initial stage will avoid time wasted and disappointment that will result if the finished garment is unsatisfactory.

Formation of Stocking Stitch

Stocking stitch is the basic fabric produced on domestic machines and a knowledge of how it is formed will help you to prevent and rectify mistakes. When working in stocking stitch the purl side is facing towards you, and the knit side is facing away from you. The knit side is generally used as the right side of the work. The main parts of the knitting machine are the needle bed which holds the individual latch needles, and the knit carriage that can slide across the needle bed.

The Latch Needle

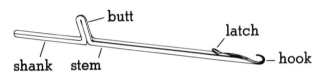

The knit carriage controls the movement of the latch needles. There are four basic needle positions and these positions are usually marked by letters or numbers at the sides of the needle bed.

Needle Positions

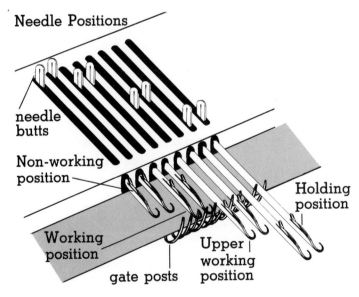

In the Non-Working Position the needles cannot be used for knitting. They will not move when the knit carriage passes over them. The needles have to be brought forward to Working Position in order to knit. Stitches can be made to 'hold' on needles in holding position until released. Consult your manual to find out how to do this. Manually bringing forward needles with tight stitches on them to holding position can also help the knit carriage run more smoothly. Your manual will give a more detailed description of the needle positions as they vary slightly from model to model.

Formation of an Individual Stitch

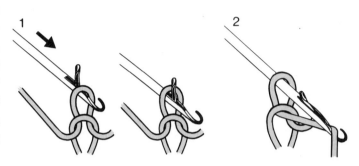

1. As the needle is moved forward, the stitch moves back, opening the latch and slipping behind it.

2. The knit carriage moves across the needle laying yarn in the open latch.

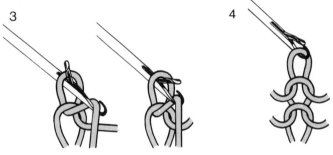

3. The needle then moves back, the old stitch moves forward and closes the latch over the yarn in the hook.

4. The needle returns to Working Position, the old stitch slides over the latch and off the needle. The yarn in the hook is pulled through to form a new stitch.

The Latch Tool

The best way to see the action of the latch needle is to move it by hand. Once you are familiar with the way stitches are formed it should be much easier to pick up and knit dropped stitches with the latch tool. Also, half-knitted rows caused by the carriage jamming should no longer be a problem as they can be finished off by hand.

Methods of Cast On
Open Edge Cast On

This method is quick and simple, making it ideal for tension or test pieces as it produces an unfinished edge that will unravel. It can also be used for garment pieces that have to be grafted together or where the edge is subsequently hooked back onto the needles to make a hem. In this case waste yarn should be used for cast on and to knit several rows before changing to main yarn.

1. Push forward required number of needles to Working Position.

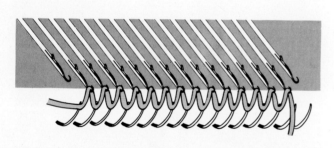

2. With yarn in the feeder, move carriage across the needle bed once. The yarn should be caught alternately between gate posts and needles. It is important that all the needles return to working position with no uneven loops at the edge.

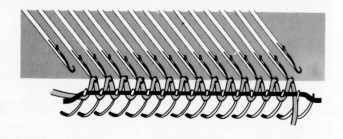

3. Lay a nylon cord (available from machine stockists) across the loops as shown.

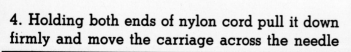

4. Holding both ends of nylon cord pull it down firmly and move the carriage across the needle bed slowly. Knit 3 or 4 rows before releasing nylon cord. Cast on is complete.

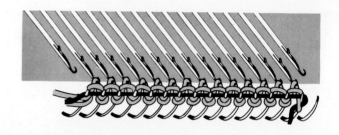

Closed Edge Cast On

This method produces a finished edge that does not unravel.

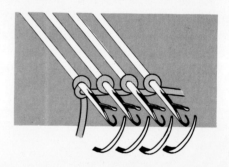

1. With carriage at right push forward required number of needles to Holding Position.

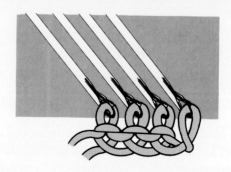

2. Fasten yarn to left end needle and loop it in an anti-clockwise direction around each needle. It is important to make the loops even. Push loops back to the stems of the needle behind the latches.

3. Thread the yarn into feeder, taking up any slack by hand. Move the carriage across needle bed slowly. Return needles to Holding Position for the first 2 to 4 rows of knitting.

Increasing

To increase one stitch at the edge of the knitting simply move the needle forward into working position. When the carriage is moved across the needle bed the empty needle will pick up the yarn and form a new stitch.

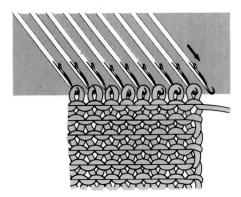

To increase several stitches on the carriage side push the needles to be increased into holding position. Wind yarn around needles as for the closed edge cast on. Take up slack yarn by hand and move carriage across needle bed slowly. Return needles to Holding Position for the first 2 to 4 rows of knitting.

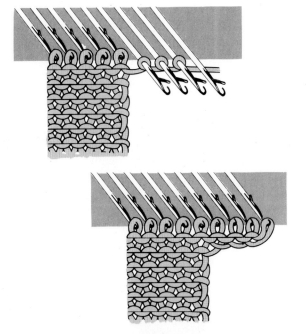

Methods of Cast Off
Open Edge Cast Off

This method is quick and simple but it produces an unfinished edge that will unravel, making it ideal for tension pieces. By changing to waste yarn several rows before casting off, and after main knitting is completed, this method can be used for garment pieces that have to be grafted together or where two pieces can be hooked onto the needles and cast off together (see Closed Edge Cast Off). Remove waste yarn from feeder and move carriage across needle bed. The knitting will then drop from the machine. For this reason care must be taken that yarn does not get accidently removed from the feeder.

Closed Edge Cast Off

This method produces a finished edge that does not unravel.

The Transfer Tool

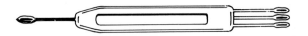

1. Using transfer tool, transfer end stitch nearest carriage to adjacent needle away from carriage. Push this needle forward to Holding Position. Return empty needle to Non-Working Position.

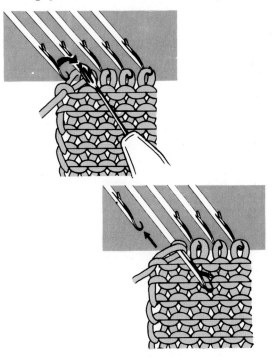

2. Lay yarn into the empty hook.

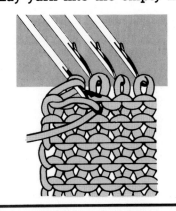

3. Hold yarn down and push the needle back to Working Position. The 2 stitches will slip off the needle, leaving a new stitch.

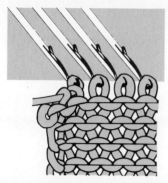

4. Continue this procedure until left with one stitch. Break yarn and draw through remaining stitch to fasten off.

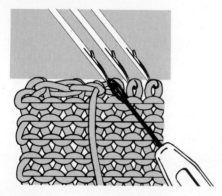

Decreasing

To decrease 1 stitch at the edge of the knitting simply transfer st to adjacent needle using transfer tool. Return empty needle to Non-Working Position before passing carriage over needle bed.

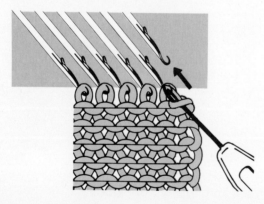

To decrease several stitches, finish with carriage on side where stitches are to be decreased. Decrease the required number of stitches using the same method as for Closed Edge Cast Off.

Joining and Finishing
Grafting

Two pieces of knitting that have 'Open Edges' can be joined invisibly by grafting.

1. Lay the pieces to be joined close together, with the stitches on either side corresponding to those opposite. Thread a wool or tapestry needle with the knitting yarn and pass it through the right end stitch.

2. Pass the needle through the first stitch of the upper piece.

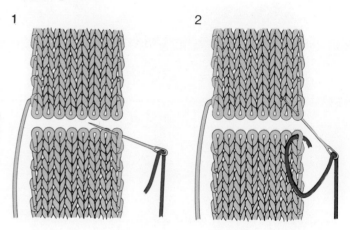

3. Pass it down through the first stitch of the lower piece then bring it up through the next stitch to the left.

4. Pass it down through the first stitch of the upper piece then bring it up through the next stitch to the left.

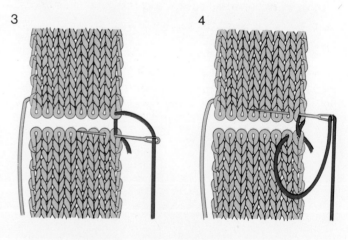

5. Repeat steps 3 and 4 with 2nd, 3rd and subsequent stitches.

Mattress Stitch Seam

This type of seam gives the neatest, most professional finish.

1. Lay the pieces to be joined close together, with the rows on either side corresponding to those opposite. Thread a wool or tapestry needle with the knitting yarn. Pass the needle under the top two 'bars' on the right side.

2. Repeat this on the left side.

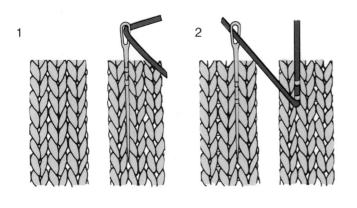

3. Return to the first side and pass the thread under the next two 'bars', repeating this first on one side and then on the other until a few stitches have been worked.

4. Pull the thread firmly so that the stitches are held together quite tightly. Stretch the seam slightly to give the required amount of elasticity, then continue with the next section of seam.

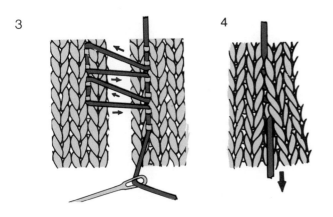

Mattress stitch can be worked either one stitch in from the edge as in the diagrams, or half a stitch in from the edge according to how neat the edge of the fabric is and how thick the yarn is. Where

the knit side of the work is the right side, work under two rows (bars) at a time as shown, where purl is used as the right side it is better to work under only one row at a time.

One advantage of mattress stitch is that it can be used to sew shaped edges together quite easily; because you are working on the right side of the work all the time it is much easier to see where you are and to keep the seam neat.

Punchcards

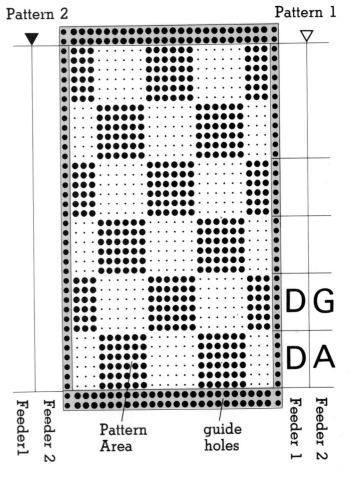

Punchcards are used to programme the machine for patterning. The holes and blanks on the cards determine which needles are selected to knit pattern stitches. The stitch patterns on the following pages have been designed specifically for machines that use punchcards with a maximum repeat of 24 stitches. However, they can be adapted for use with models that have a different maximum repeat. The pattern area of the punch-card can be transferred directly onto graph paper for use with elecronic machines. The patterns can be worked on non-automatic machines by hand selecting needles across the entire width of the fabric. Guide holes should be ignored when hand selecting needles for patterning.

To make your own pattern cards you will need blank punchcards and a hand punch, available from machine stockists. The holes to be punched should be marked first with pencil. All punchcards should start and finish with 2 rows of guide holes as shown. These enable the card to be clipped together without obscuring any of the pattern. Care should be taken to punch the cards exactly as shown. If a mistake is made it is possible to re-cover a wrongly punched hole by attaching a small piece of adhesive tape to the back and front of the card, being careful not to obscure any of the cor-rect holes.

Once the punchcard has been made it will be eas-ier to use if the row numbers are marked on it. Refer to the manual to find out how to number the card so that when row 1 is shown, the row being knitted corresponds with the bottom row of the dia-gram. It is important to start knitting at row 1 when following the colour changes given at the side of the diagrams. See your machine manual for details of **your** machine.

Diagrams include suggested colours and these have been indicated by a letter shown on the colour chart below.

How to Read Punchcard Diagrams

To knit the fairisle sample shown on previous page (∇), set the card to start knitting at row 1 and referring to your manual, set the machine to knit fairisle.
Place **D** in feeder 1 and **A** in feeder 2.
Knit 6 rows.
Keeping **D** in feeder 1, replace **A** in feeder 2 with **G.**
Knit 6 rows.
Repeat these 12 rows.

If there is no yarn shown in a particular feeder leave it empty to knit the required number of rows.

Where two patterns have been knitted using one punchcard, triangle symbols have been used to indicate the colour changes that correspond with the patterns.

Colour Chart
The colours shown are approximate equivalents to yarn colours used in the samples.

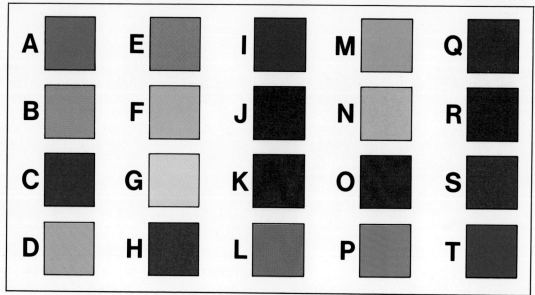

Fairisle is a stocking stitch fabric where two colours are used in the same row. One set of needles corresponding to the blank spaces on the punchcard knits the yarn in feeder 1. The second set of needles corresponding to the holes on the punchcard knits the yarn in feeder 2.

On non-automatic machines selected needles usually knit the yarn in feeder 2. See your machine manual to confirm the method for your machine. Needles corresponding to the holes in the punchcard should be selected across the entire width of the fabric. You may find it helpful to place a ruler underneath the row you are working on the diagram.

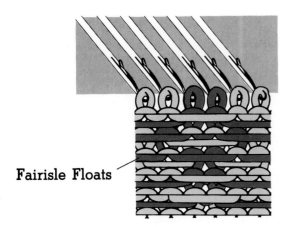

Fairisle Floats

The yarn not in use makes a 'float' along the wrong side of the work. Long floats can cause problems in knitted fabric that is not lined. It is therefore better not to have too many stitches in the same colour along one row of fairisle knitting.

When knitting rows that consist of one colour only within a fairisle pattern it is important that the machine end needle selector mechanism is not in use. (It will cause the 2nd colour to knit the first and last stitches only thus giving a float across the entire width of the fabric).

Patterns with more than two Colours

To prevent cutting and rejoining yarn continuously do not thread the extra colours through the top tension discs of the machine. Keep the yarn at the side of the machine and feed it by hand.

Motifs

Motifs are fairisle patterns worked over a limited area. Consult your manual for details on how to set your machine to knit single motifs. As motifs only cover a small area, it is acceptable to have longer floats.

I. Fairisle

Punchcard instructions and colour key on pages 9 and 10.

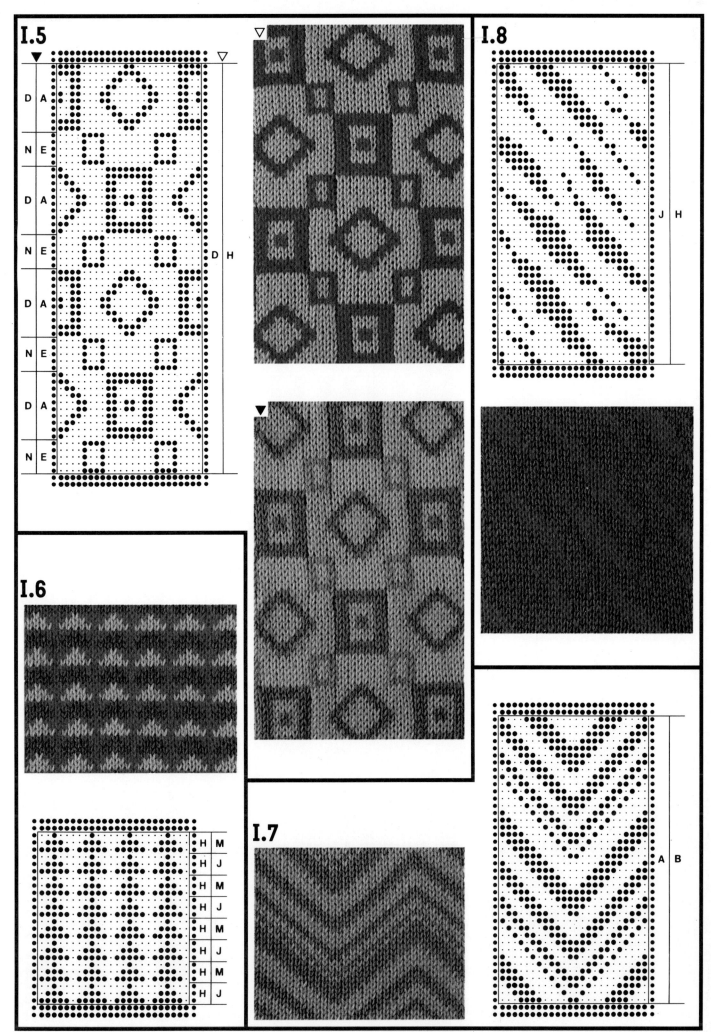

I.5

I.6

I.7

I.8

13

I. Fairisle

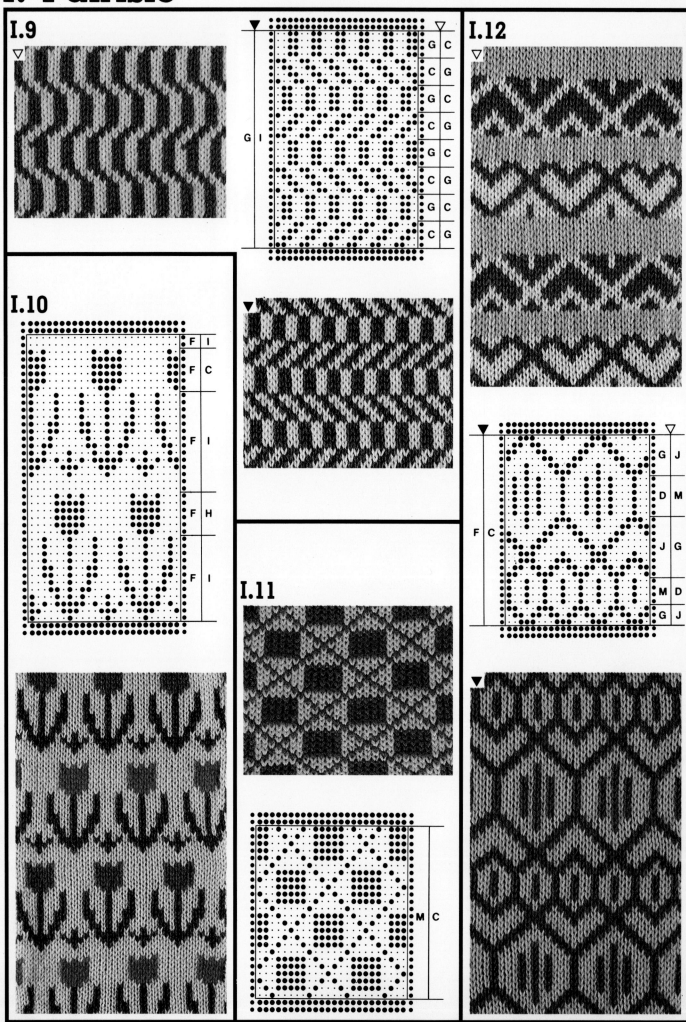

I.9

I.10

		F	I
		F	C
		F	I
		F	H
		F	I

I.11

| | M | C |

I.12

	G	C
	C	G
	G	C
	C	G
	C	G
G	I	C	C
	C	C
	G	C
	C	G

	G	J
	D	M
F	C	J	G
	M	D
	G	J

Punchcard instructions and colour key on pages 9 and 10.

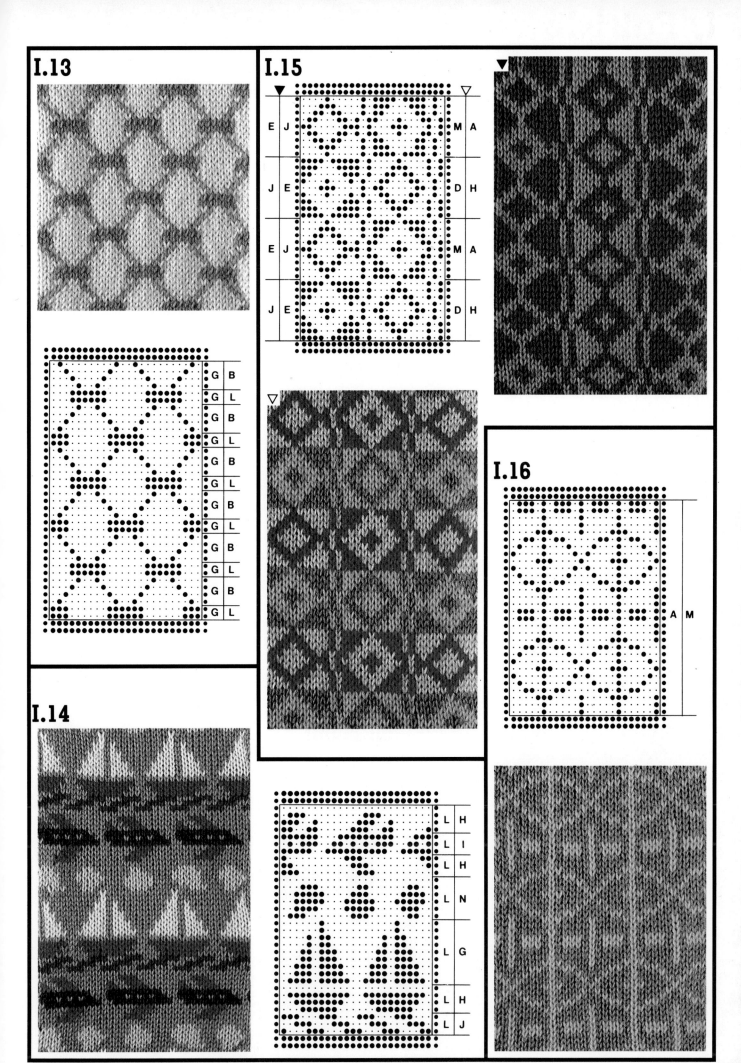

I. Fairisle

I.17

G	I
G	I H
G	I
G	I H
G	B
G	I
G	I H
G	I
G	B
G	I
G	I H
G	I
G	B
G	I
G	I H
G	I
G	B

I.19

A	L
C	J
L	D
J	G
D	A
G	C

I.18

I	M

I.20

	A	M
	A	C
A H	A	M
	A	C
	A	M

I.21

D	B
G	L
D	B
G	L
D	B
G	L
D	B
G	L
D	B

B J

I.22

D	G
D	A
D	G
D	A
D	G
D	A

I.23

G J

I.24

D	A
E	D
D	A
F	E
A	F
D	A
E	D
D	A
F	E
A	F

I. Fairisle

I.25

I.26

I.27

Punchcard instructions and colour key on pages 9 and 10.

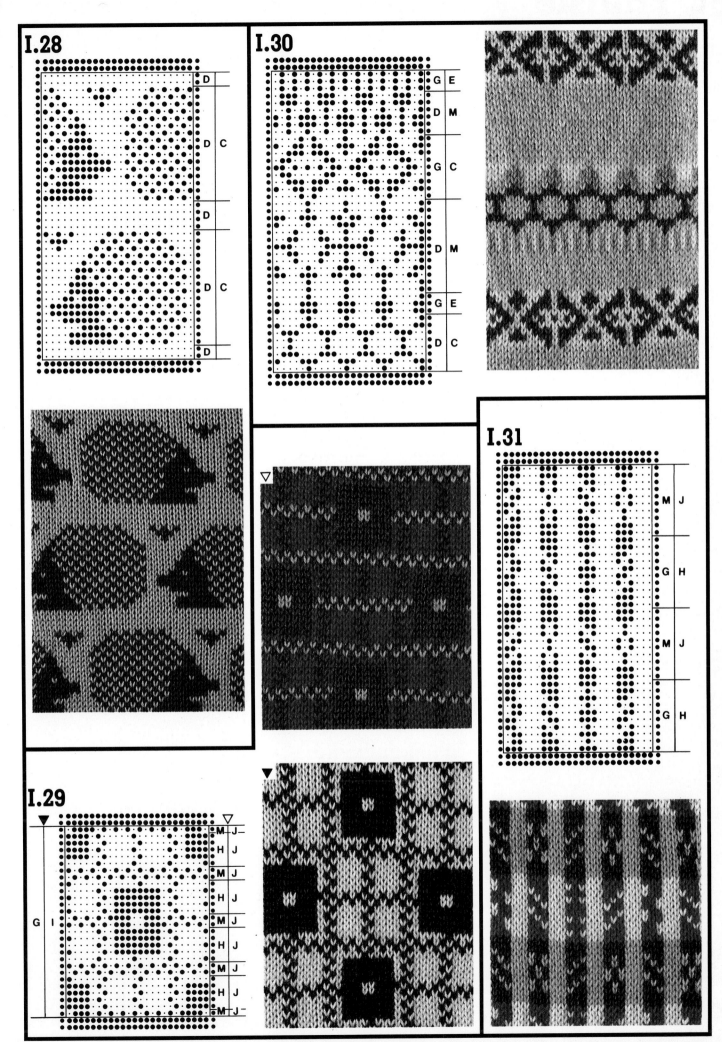

I. Fairisle

I.32

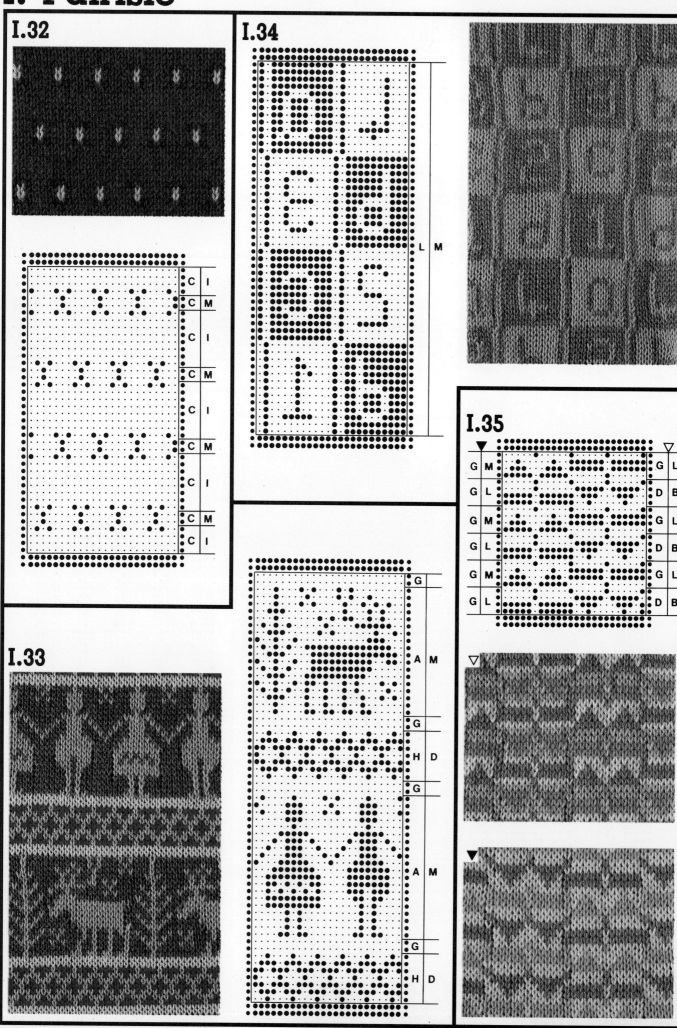

I.34

I.33

I.35

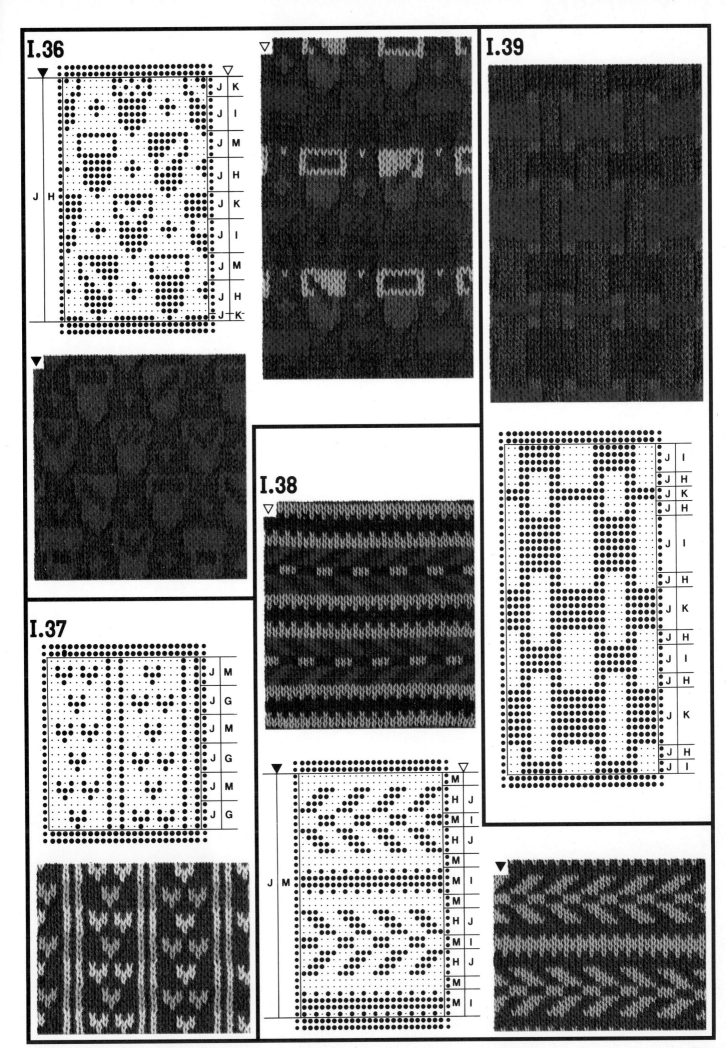

I. Fairisle

I.40

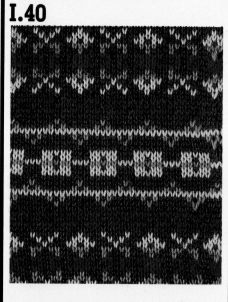

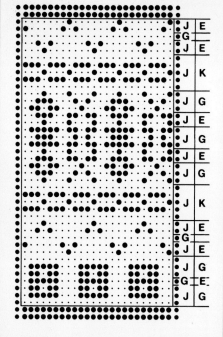

	J	E
	G	E
	J	E
	J	K
	J	G
	J	E
	J	G
	E	G
	J	G
	J	K
	J	E
	G	E
	J	E
	J	G
	G	E
	J	G

I.42

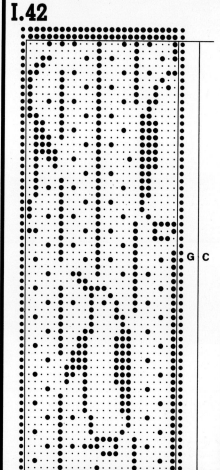

G | C

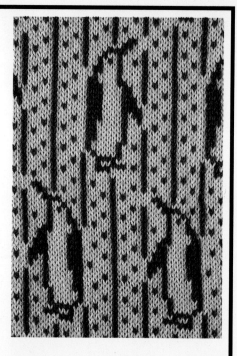

I.43

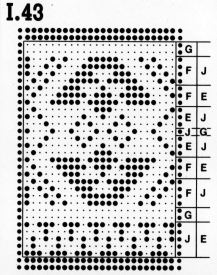

	G	
	F	J
	F	E
	E	J
	J	G
	E	J
	F	E
	F	J
	G	
	J	E

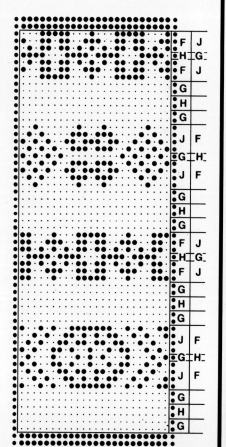

	F	J
	H	G
	F	J
	G	
	H	
	G	
	J	F
	G	H
	J	F
	G	
	H	
	G	
	F	J
	H	G
	F	J
	G	
	H	
	G	
	J	F
	G	H
	J	F
	G	
	H	
	G	

I.41

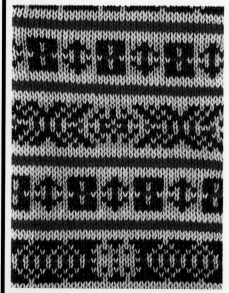

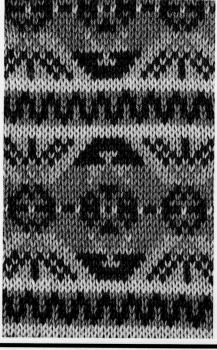

Punchcard instructions and colour key on pages 9 and 10.

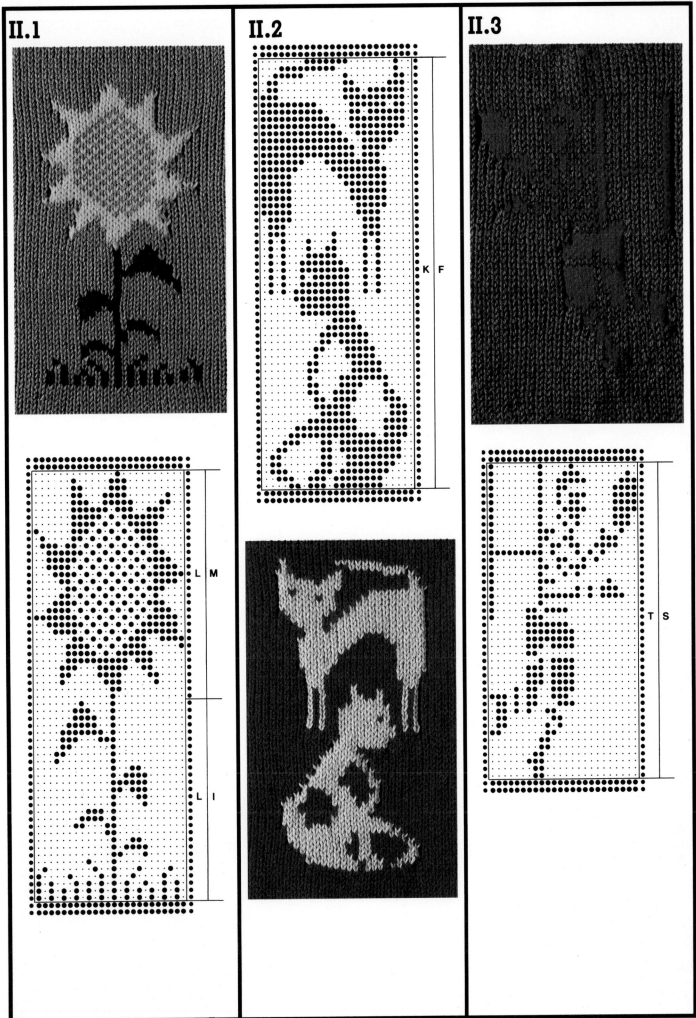

II.1

II.2

II.3

II. Motifs

II.4

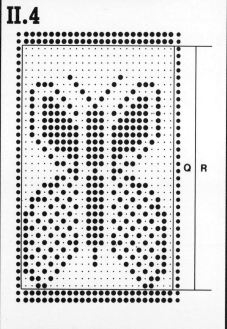

II.6

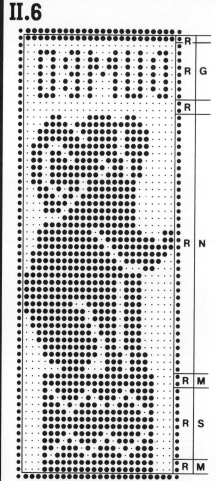

II.7

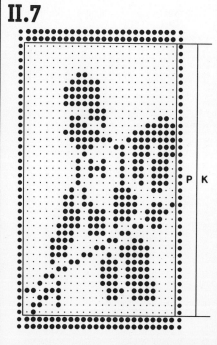

II.5

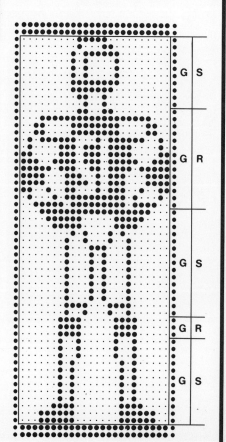

Punchcard instructions and colour key on pages 9 and 10.

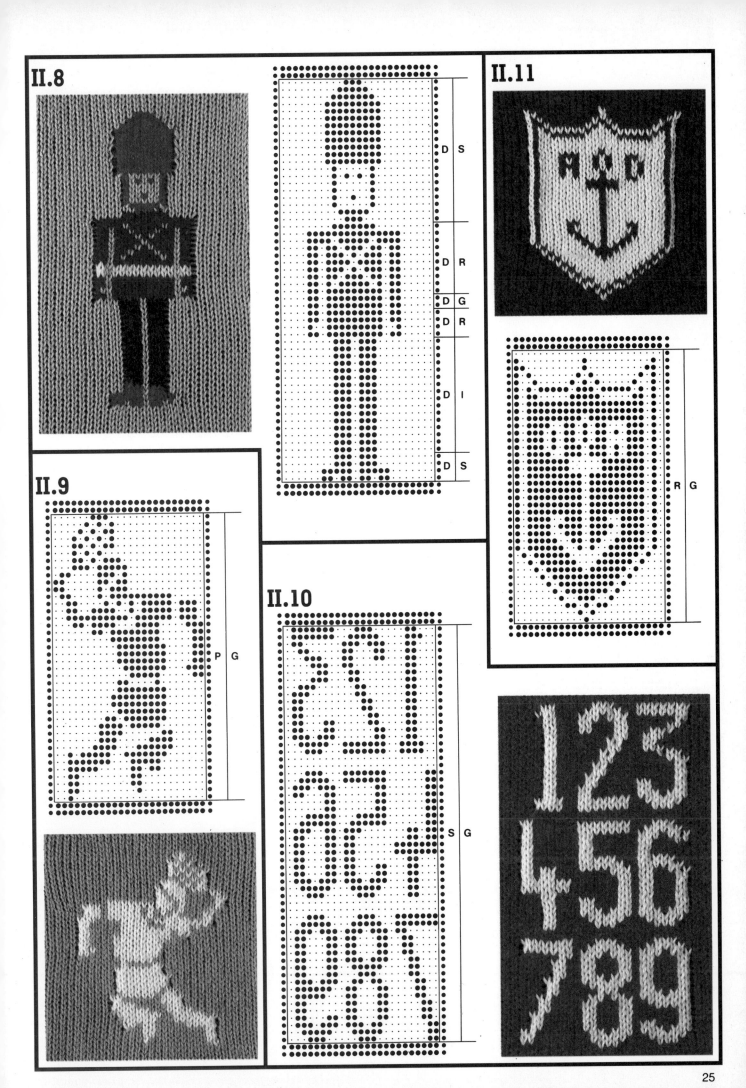

II.8

II.9

II.10

II.11

D S
D R
D G
D R

D I

D S

P G

R G

S G

II. Motifs

II.12

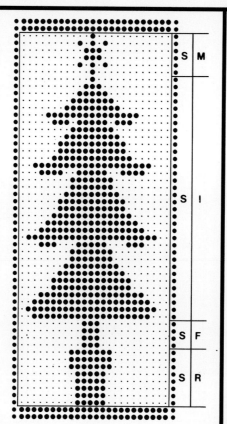

	S	M
	S	I
	S	F
	S	R

II.15

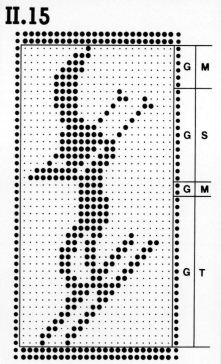

	G	M
	G	S
	G	M
	G	T

II.13

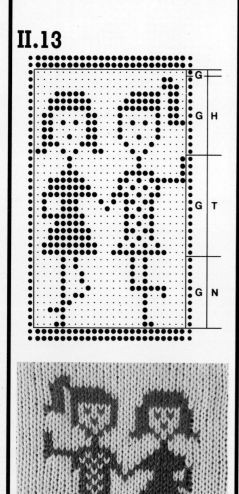

	G	
	G	H
	G	T
	G	N

II.14

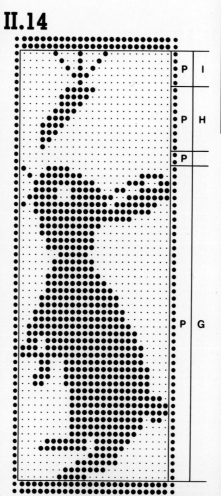

	P	I
	P	H
	P	
	P	G

Punchcard instructions and colour key on pages 9 and 10.

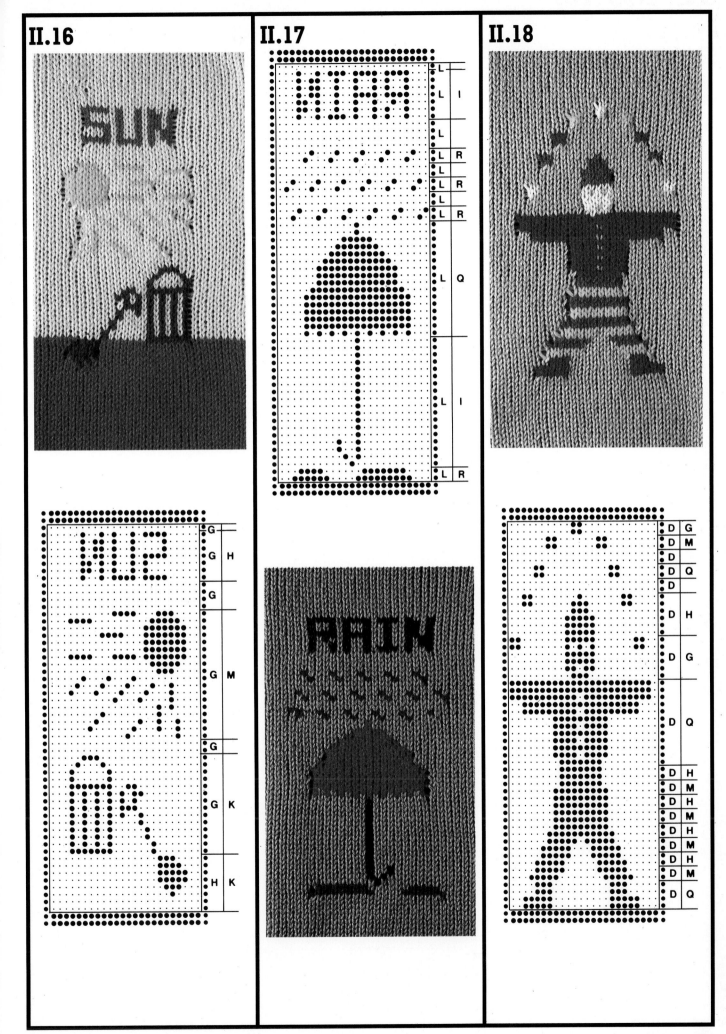

II. Motifs

II.19

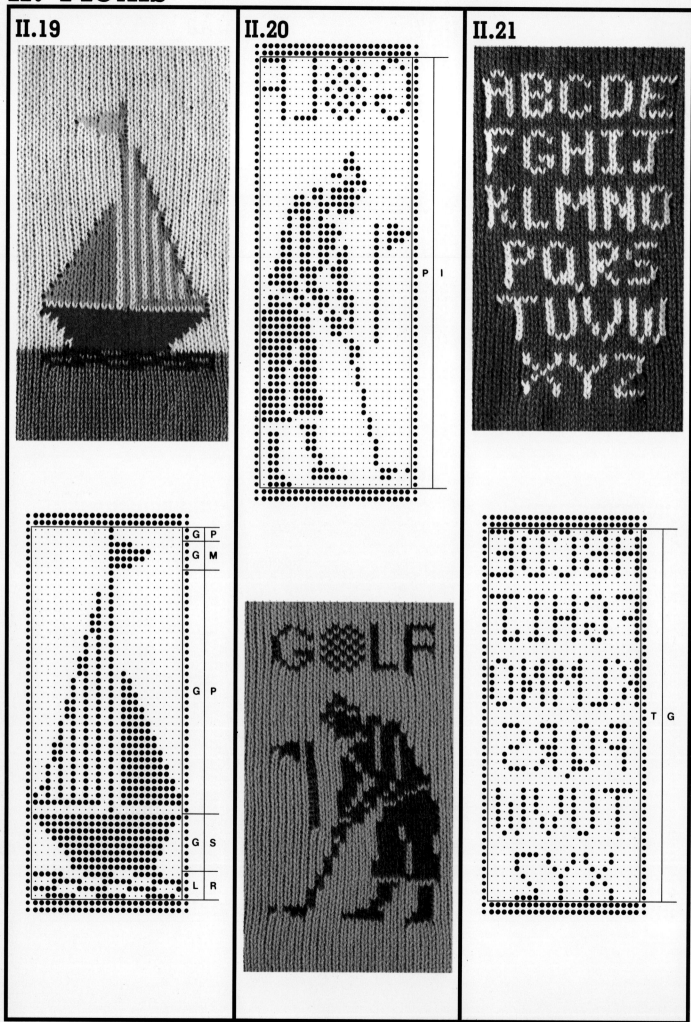

II.20

II.21

Punchcard instructions and colour key on pages 9 and 10.

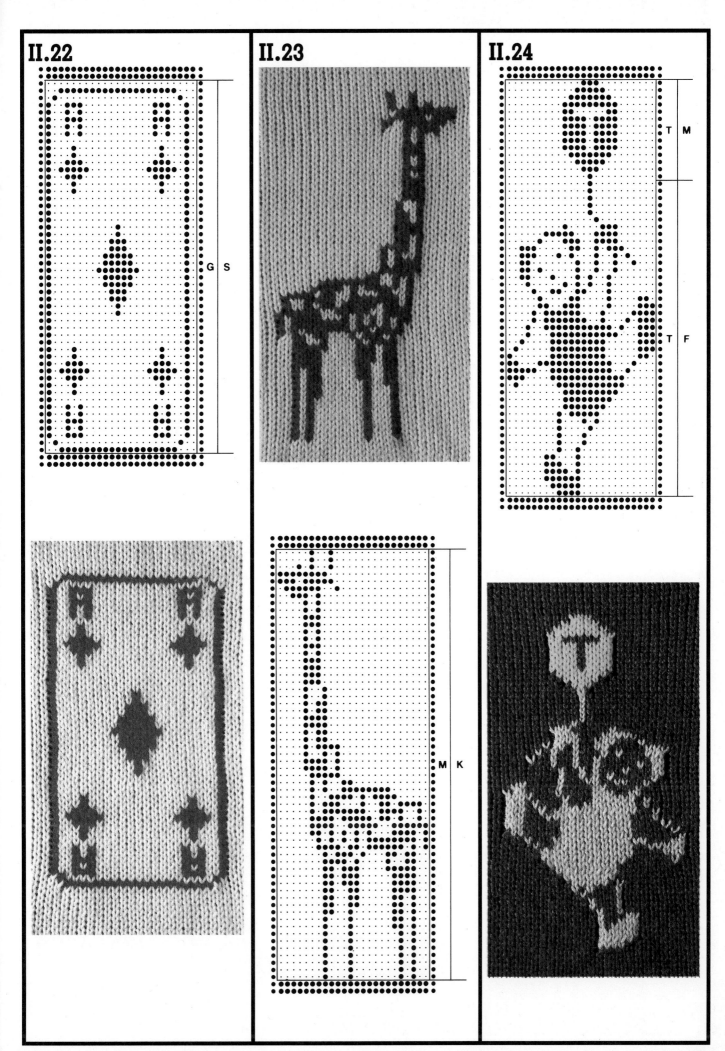

II.22

II.23

II.24

G S

T M

T F

M K

III. Tuck Stitch

The needles corresponding to the holes on the punchcard knit stocking stitch. The needles corresponding to the blank spaces on the punchcard catch a loop of yarn without actually knitting it.

On non-automatic machines selected needles usually knit stocking stitch. Therefore needles corresponding to the holes in the punchcard should be selected across the entire width of the fabric. You may find it helpful to place a ruler underneath the row you are working on the diagram.

By varying the position of the tuck stitches interesting effects can be produced on the knit side of the fabric. When some tuck stitch patterns are knitted in 2 row coloured stripes a 'maze' effect is produced on the purl side.

It is not easy to use a tuck stitch over more than three or four rows without the needles becoming overloaded with loops. When this happens stitches can drop. If this becomes a problem tightening the tension slightly should alleviate it.

Tuck Lace

An openwork effect can be created by using a tuck stitch pattern whilst leaving some needles in the Non-Working Position. Strands of yarn across spaces in tucked fabric give a mock lace effect.

When knitting Tuck Lace it is important that the machine's end needle selector mechanism is not in use (it will treat any needle with an empty needle adjacent to it as the edge of the fabric).

Fine yarn set at a loose tension gives the most open fabric. Weight the fabric well whilst knitting to avoid dropped stitches.

When preparing to knit Tuck Lace, needles marked with a circle should be pushed to Non-Working Position. Always select needles outwards from either side of centre mark on needle bed and guide.

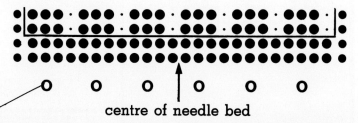

needle in non-working position   centre of needle bed

Tuck Stitch

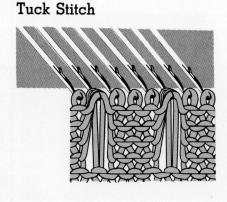

Tuck Lace

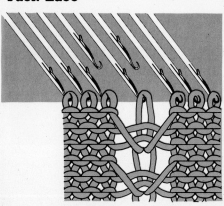

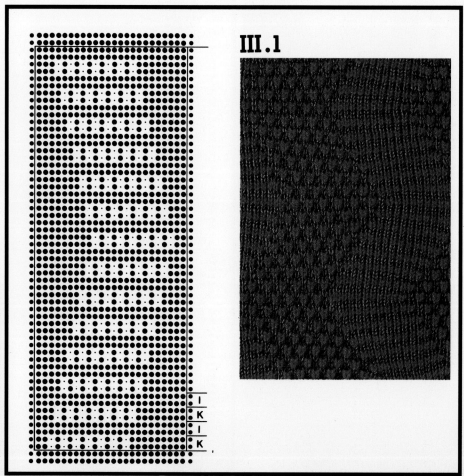

III.1

Punchcard instructions and colour key on pages 9 and 10.

III.2

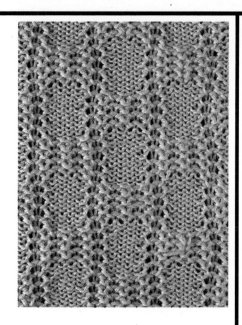

III.5

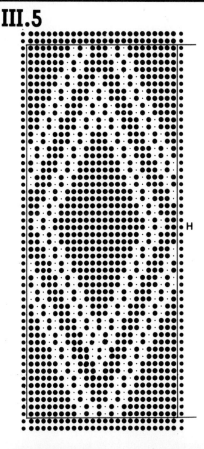

H

III.3

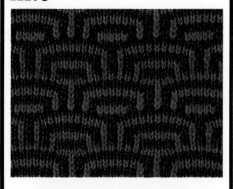

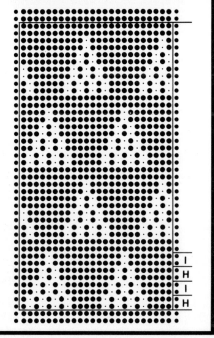

I	
H	
I	
H	

III.4

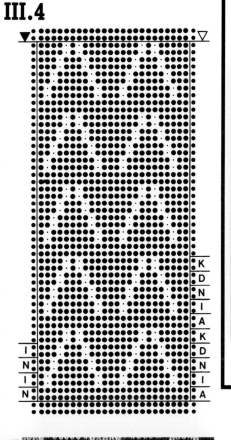

K	
D	
N	
I	
A	
K	
D	
N	
I	
A	

I	
N	
I	
N	

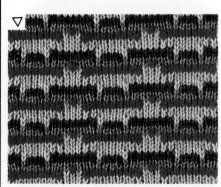

III. Tuck Stitch

III.6

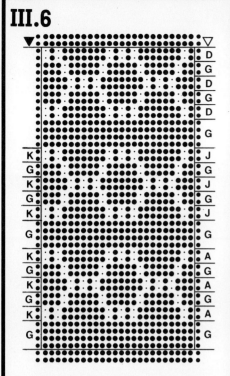

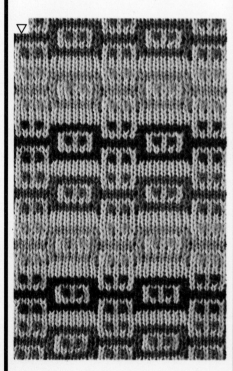

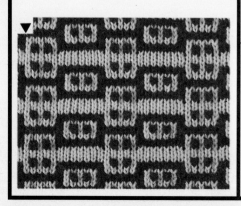

III.7

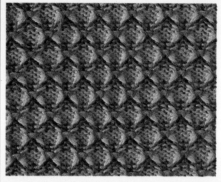

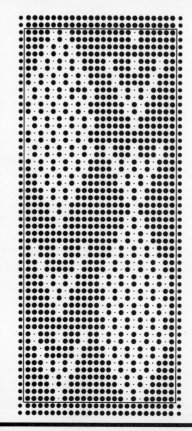

III.8

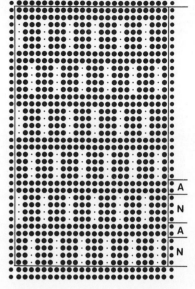

III.9

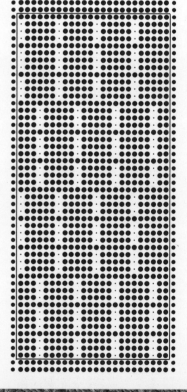

Punchcard instructions and colour key on pages 9 and 10.

III.10

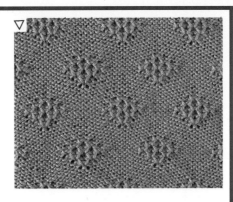

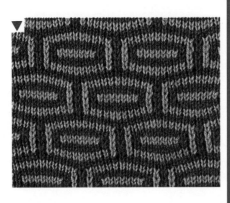

C
L
C
L

L

III.13

E

G
E
K
E
G
E
K
E

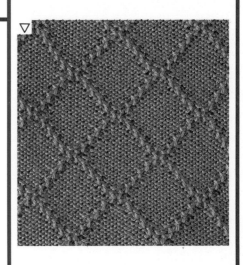

III.11

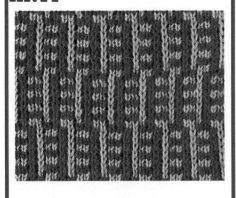

H
F
H
F

III.12

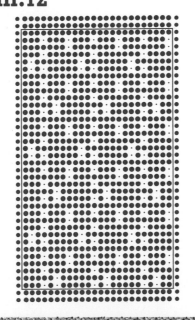

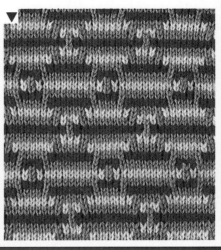

III. Tuck Stitch

III.14

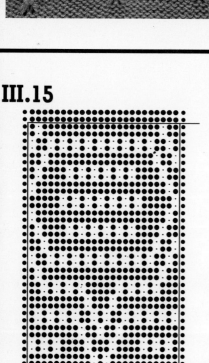

III.16

H
F
C
F
H
F
C
F

C
F
C
F

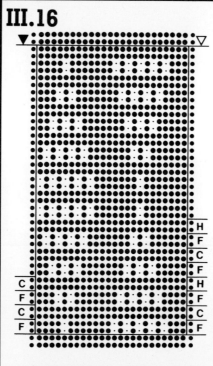

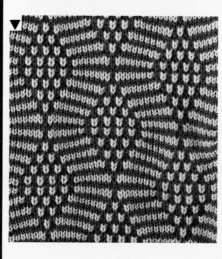

III.15

C
D
C
D

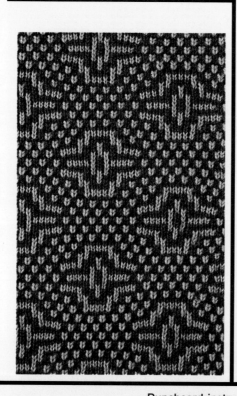

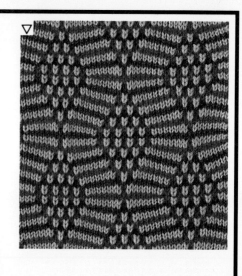

III.17

B

I
B
I
B

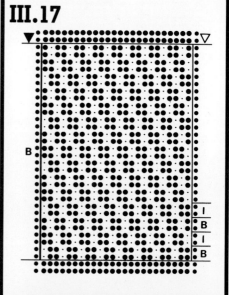

Punchcard instructions and colour key on pages 9 and 10.

III.18

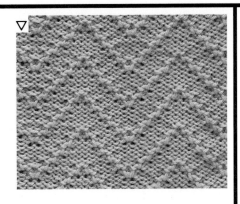

M

I
M
I
M

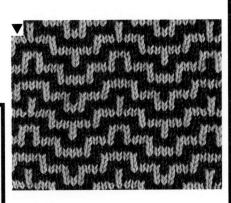

III.19

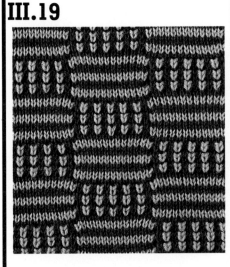

J
F
J
F

III.20

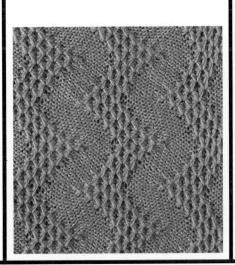

III.21

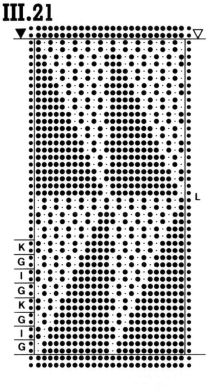

L

K
G
I
G
K
G
I
G

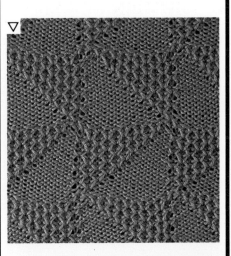

III. Tuck Stitch

III.22

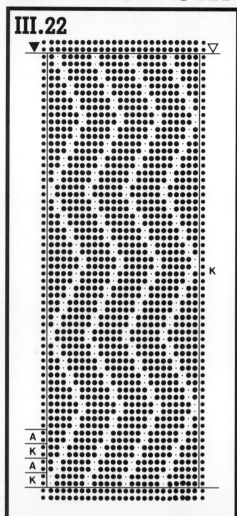

K

A
K
A
K

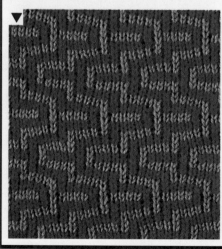

III.23

J
G
J
G
J
G
J
G
N
G
N
G
N
G

G
J
G
J

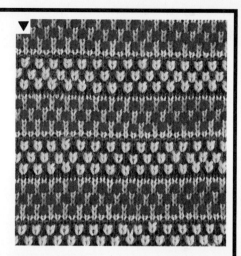

III.24

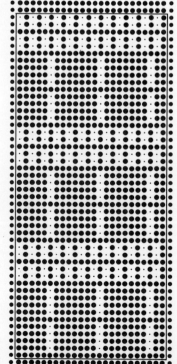

III.25

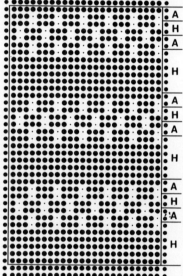

A
H
A

H

A
H
A

H

A
H
A

H

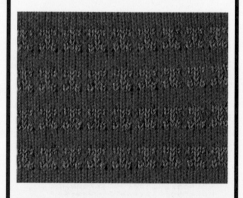

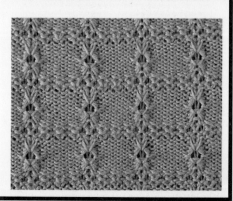

Punchcard instructions and colour key on pages 9 and 10.

III.26

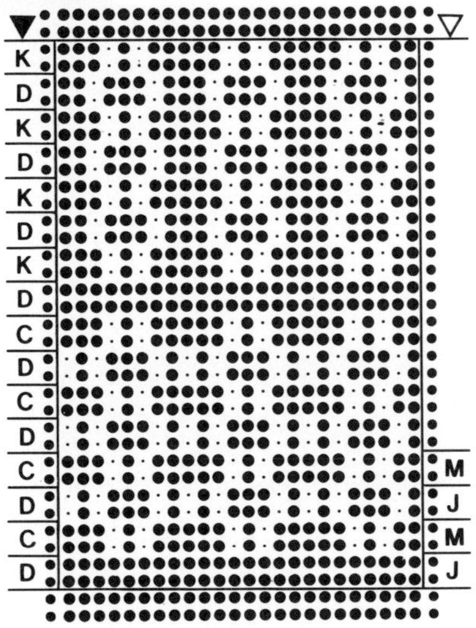
K
D
K
D
K
D
K
D
C
D
C
C
D
C
D
C
D
M
J
M
J

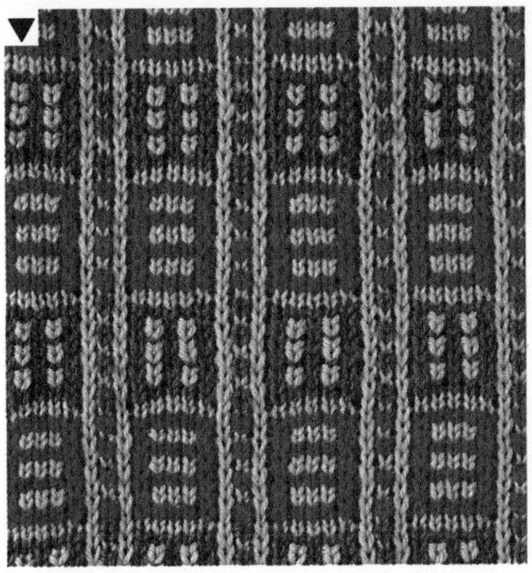

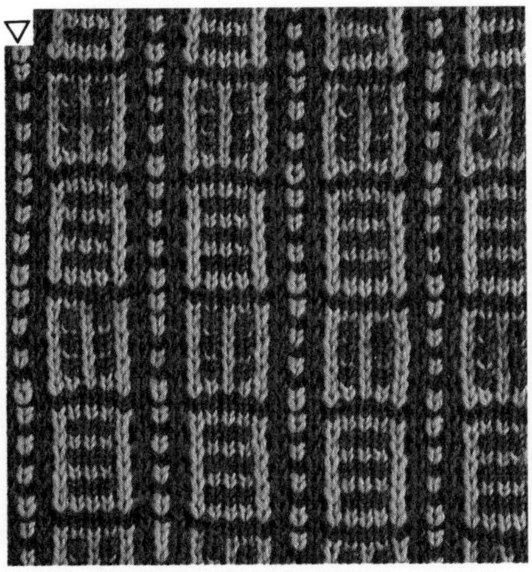

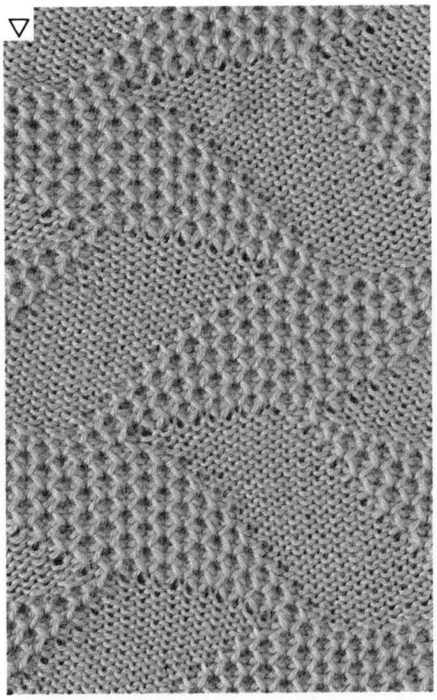

III.27

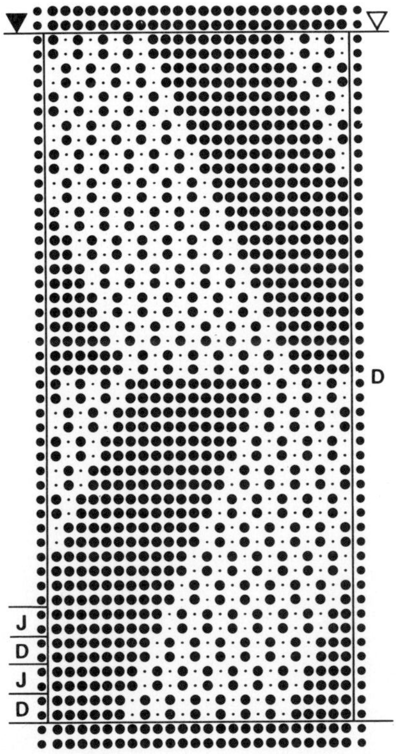
D
J
D
J
D

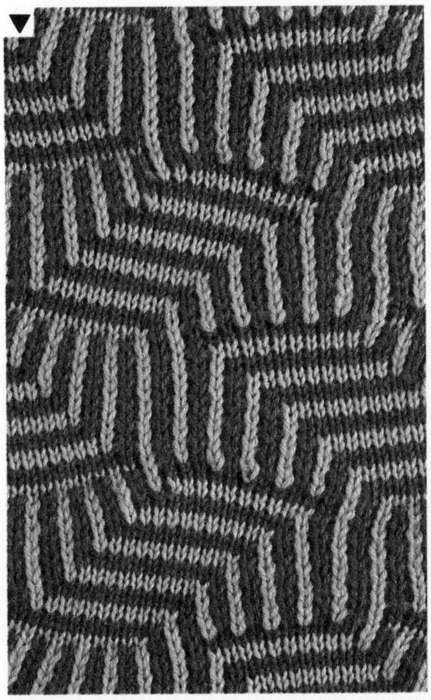

III.28

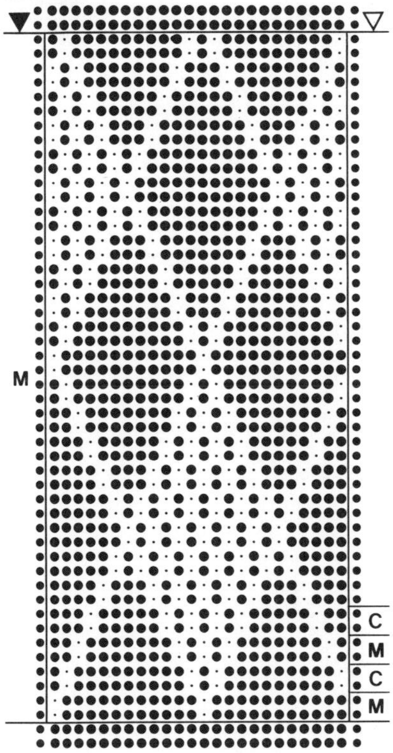
M
C
M
C
M

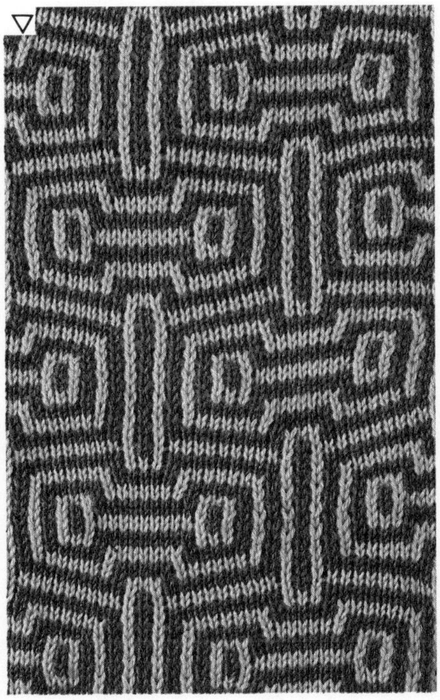

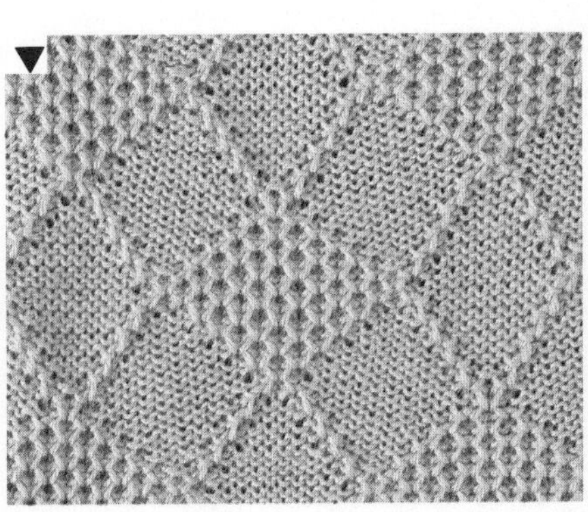

III. Tuck Stitch

III.29

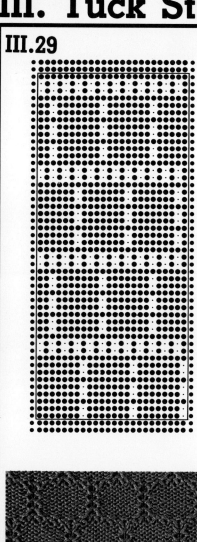

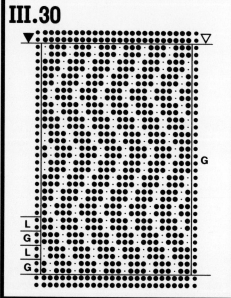

III.30

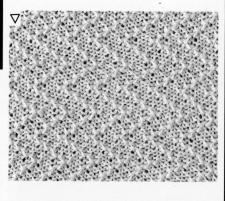

III.31

M
D
C
G
M
D
C
G

J
B
J
B

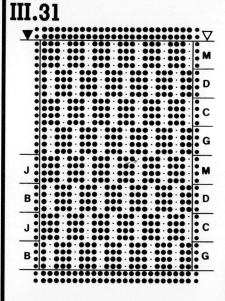

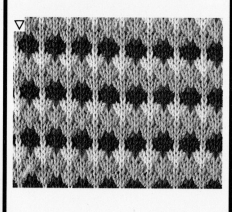

III.32

G
A
G
A

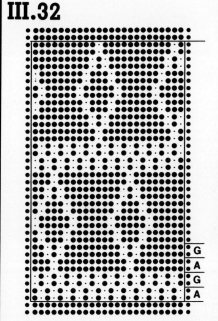

G
L
G
L
G

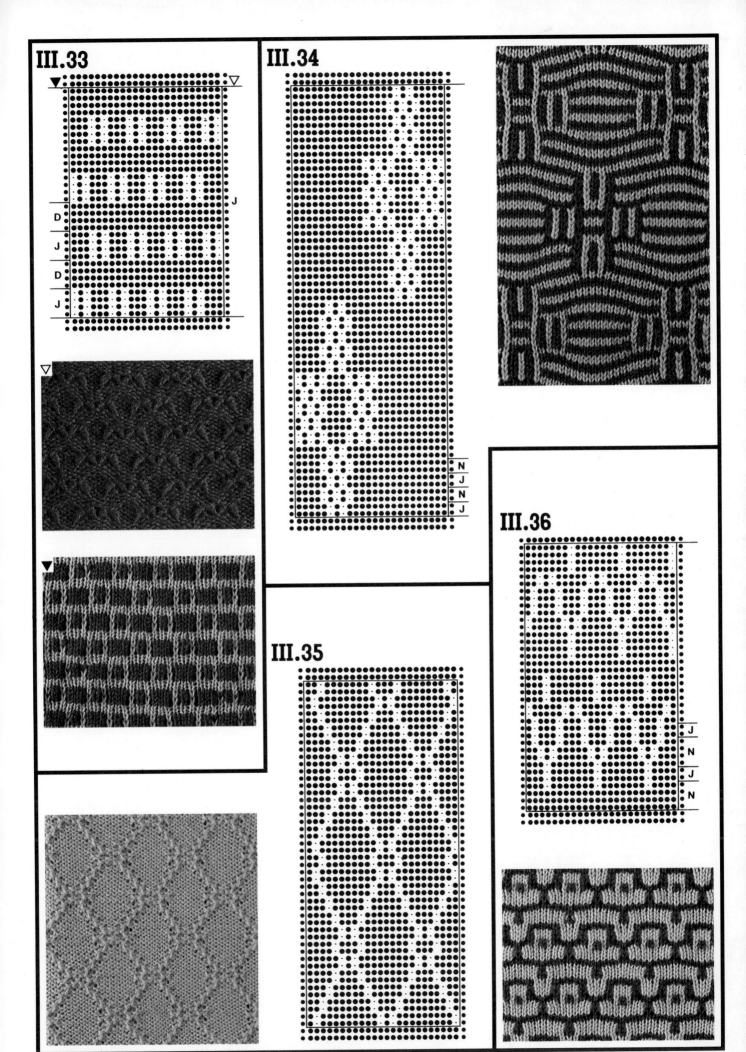

III.33

D
J
J
D
J

III.34

N
J
N
J

III.35

III.36

J
N
J
N

III. Tuck Stitch

III.37

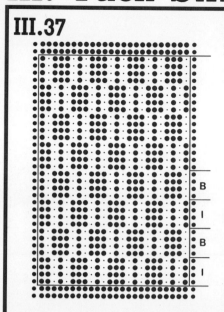

B
I
B
I

III.39

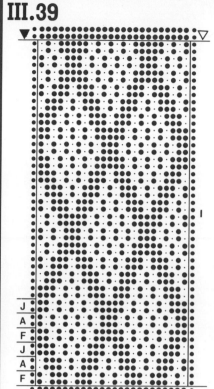

I

J
A
F
J
A
F

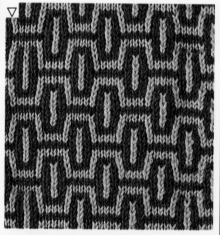

III.40

B
G
B
G

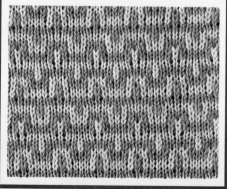

III.38

F

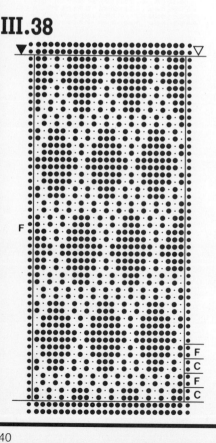

F
C
F
C

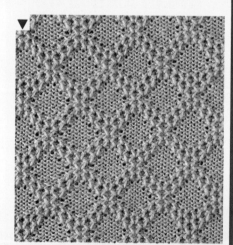

Punchcard instructions and colour key on pages 9 and 10.

III.41

M
J
M
J

III.42

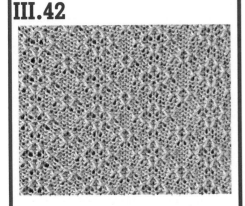

III.43

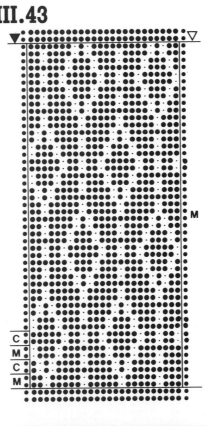

M

C
M
C
M

III.44

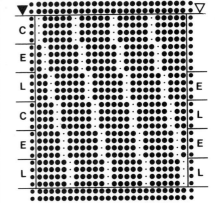

C
E
L
C
E
L

E
L
E
L

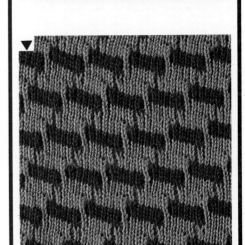

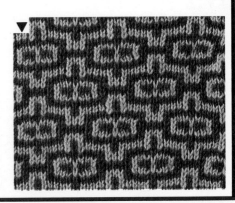

41

IV. Tuck Lace

IV.1

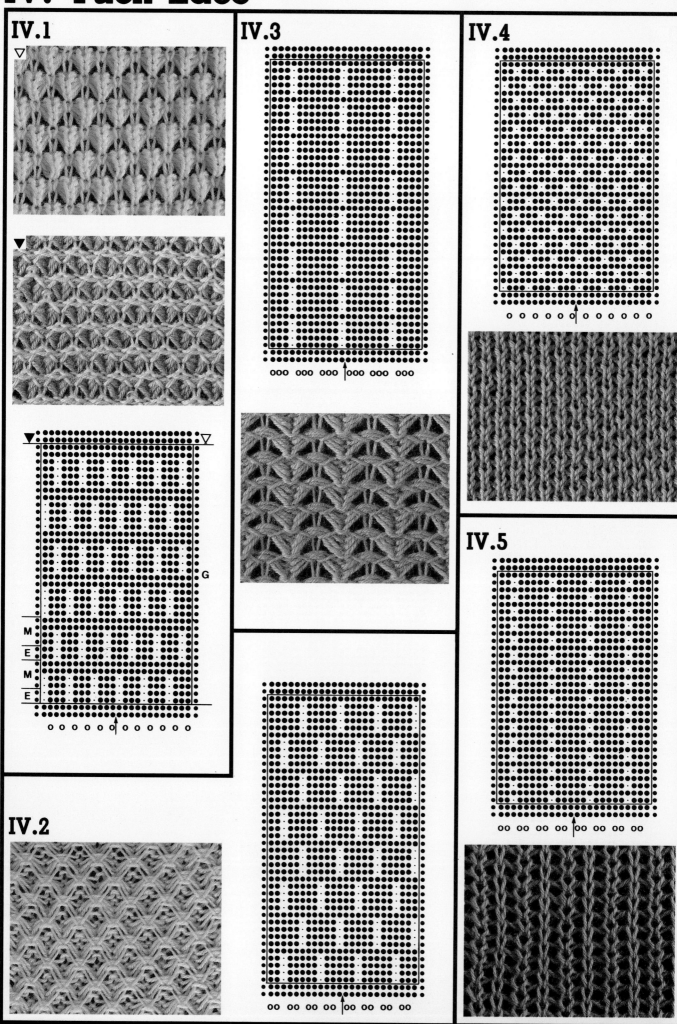

IV.2

IV.3

IV.4

IV.5

Punchcard instructions and colour key on pages 9 and 10.

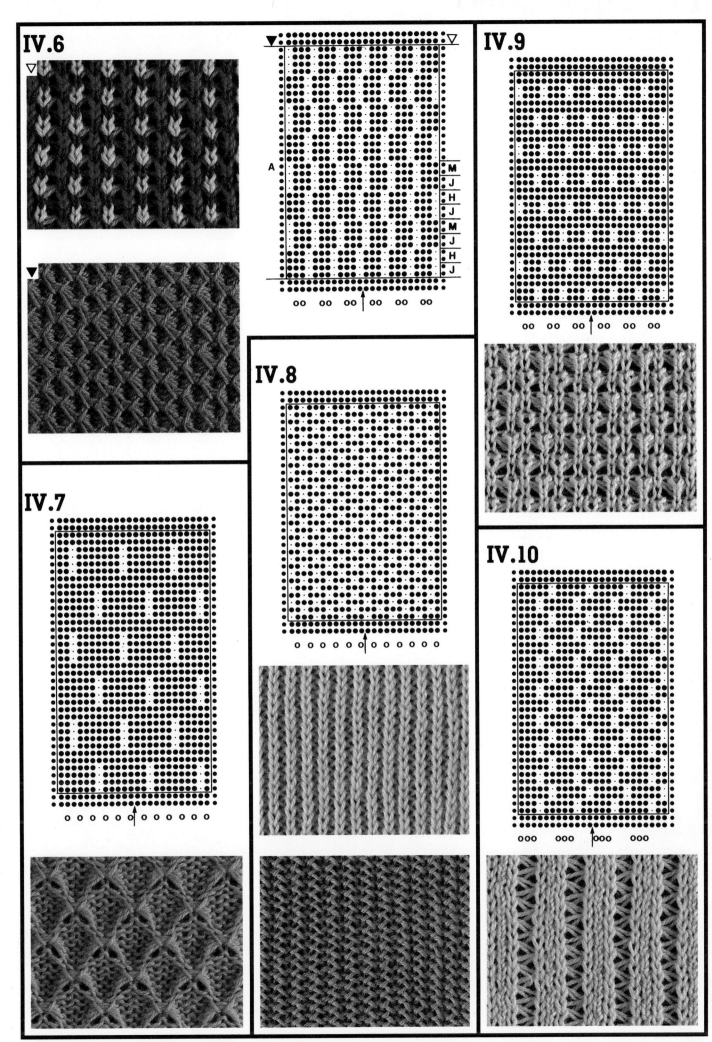

IV.6

IV.7

IV.8

IV.9

IV.10

A
M
J
H
J
M
J
H
J

IV. Tuck Lace

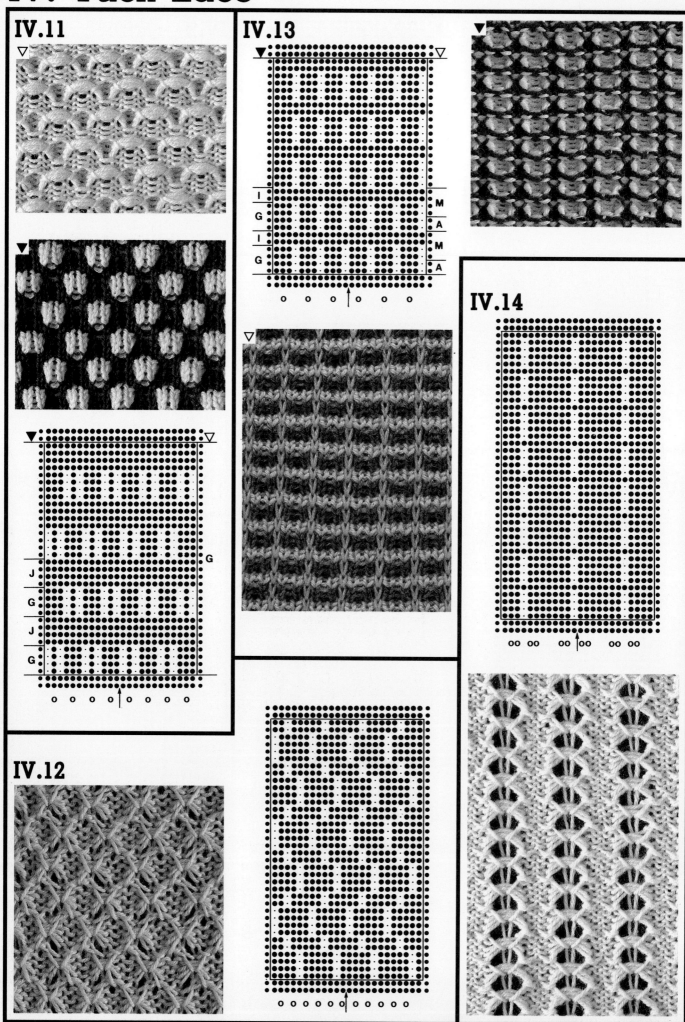

IV.11

IV.13

IV.14

IV.12

Punchcard instructions and colour key on pages 9 and 10.

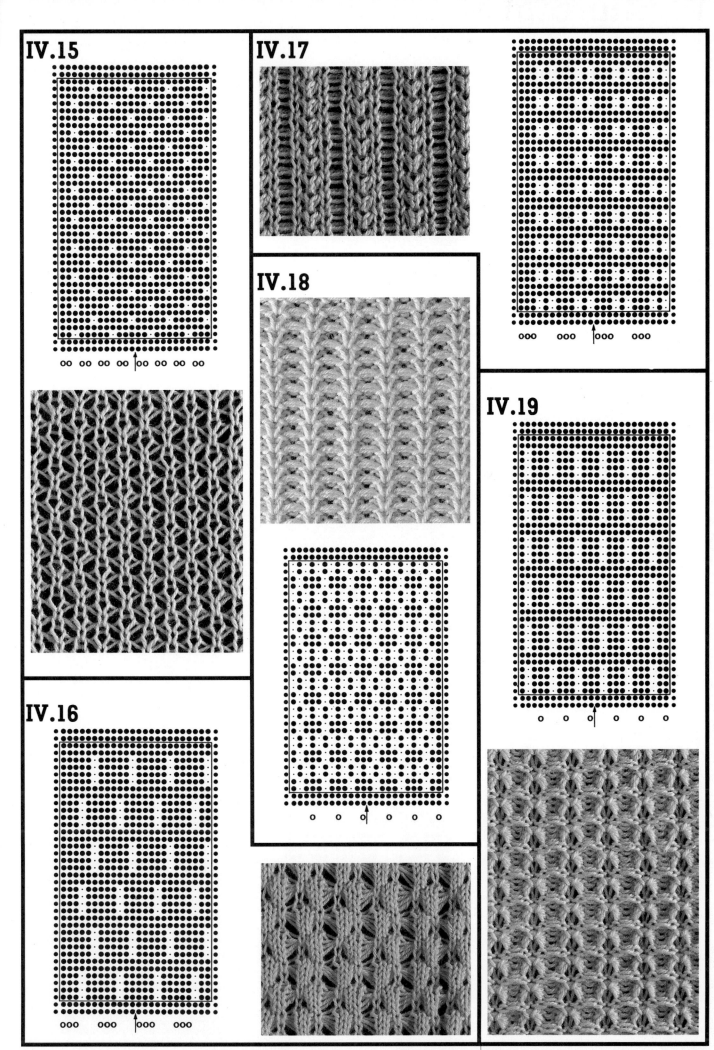

IV.15

oo   oo   oo   oo |oo   oo   oo   oo

IV.16

ooo   ooo |ooo   ooo

IV.17

IV.18

o   o   o |o   o   o

IV.19

o   o   o| o   o   o

ooo   ooo |ooo   ooo

V. Slip Stitch

The needles corresponding to the holes on the punchcard knit stocking stitch. The needles corresponding to the blank spaces on the punchcard do not move and the yarn is carried across the front of these needles.

This produces a horizontal cord effect on the purl side of the fabric. Multi-colour effects can be produced on the knit side of the fabric. However, some multi-colour slip stitch fabrics do have a large number of floats on the wrong side and this could limit their use.

On non-automatic machines selected needles usually knit stocking stitch. Therefore, needles corresponding to the holes in the punchcard should be selected across the entire width of the fabric.

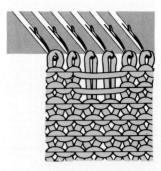

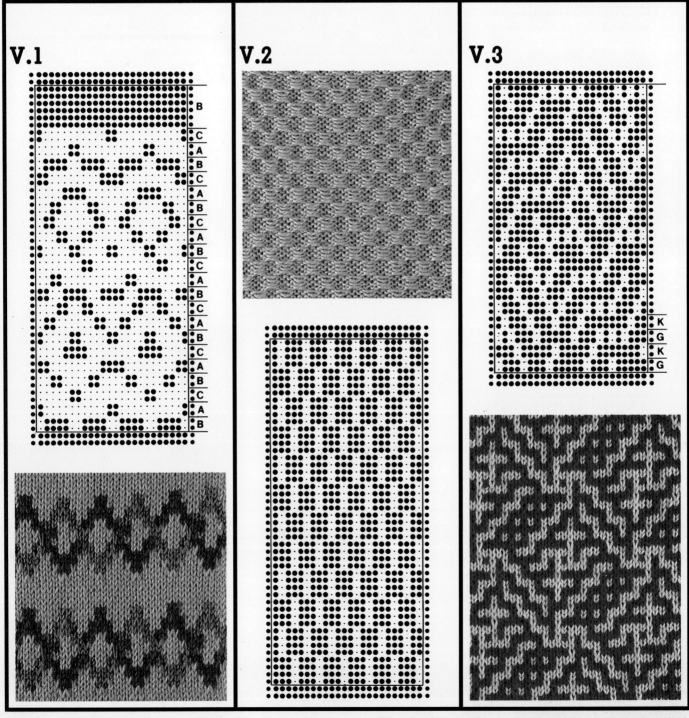

V.1

V.2

V.3

Punchcard instructions and colour key on pages 9 and 10.

V.4

V.5

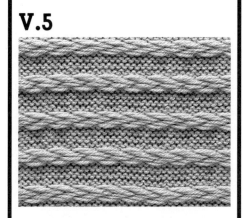

V.6

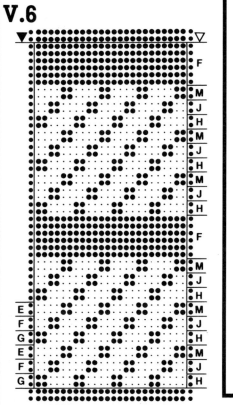

V.7

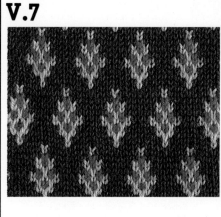

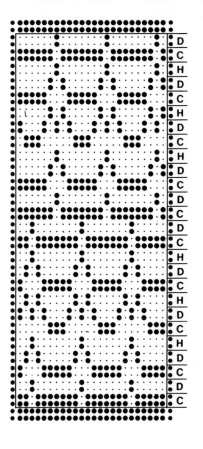

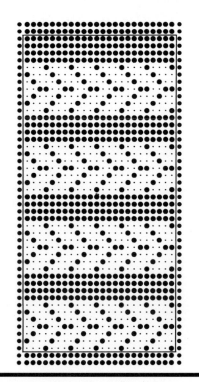

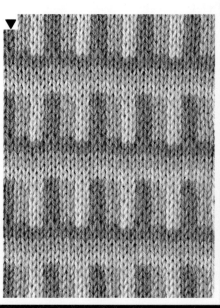

V. Slip Stitch

V.8

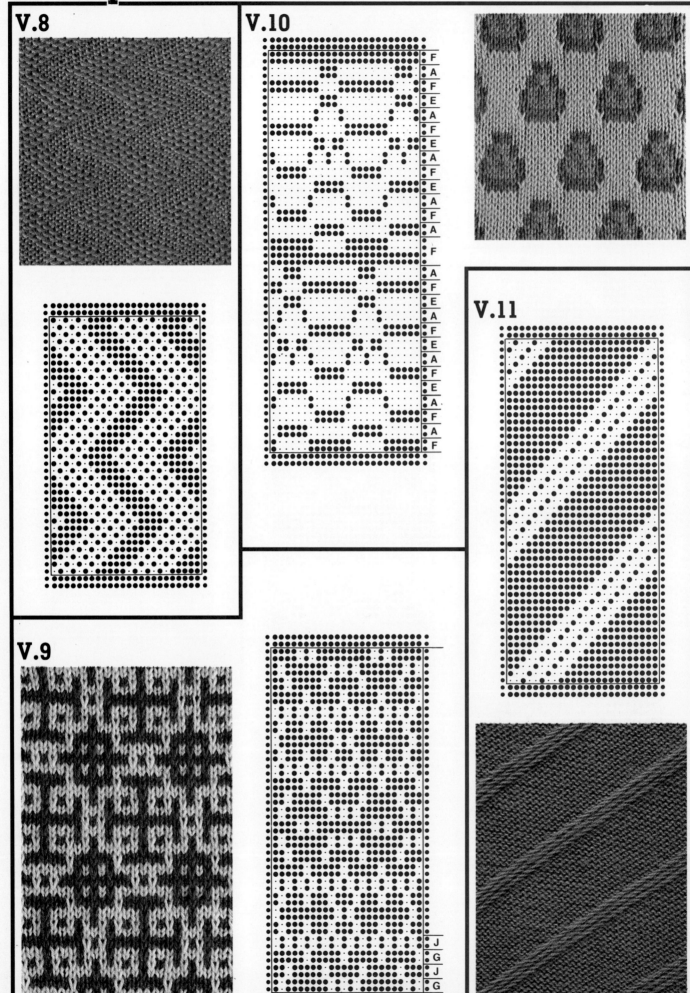

V.10

F
A
F
E
A
F
E
A
F
A
F
A
F
A
F
E
A
F
E
A
F
E
A
F
E
A
F
A
F
A
F

V.11

V.9

J
G
J
G

Punchcard instructions and colour key on pages 9 and 10.

V.12

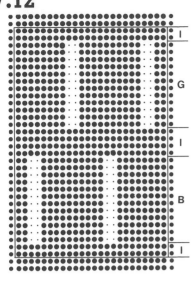

I
G
I
I
B
I

V.15

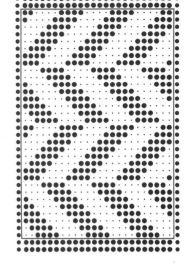

V.13

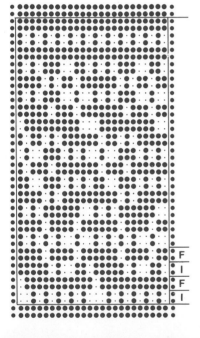

F
I
F
I

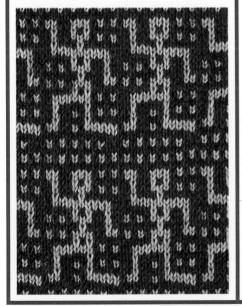

V.14

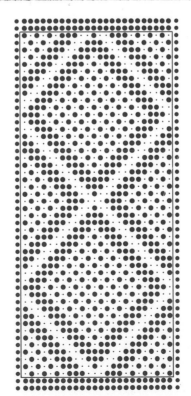

V.16

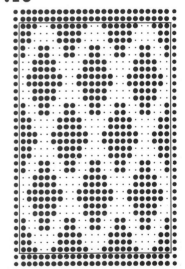

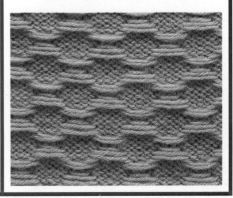

V. Slip Stitch

V.17

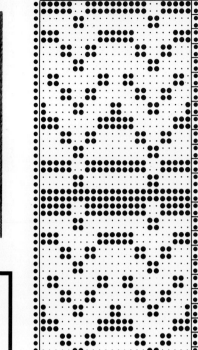

H
J
G
H
J
G
H
J
G
H
J
H
J
H
J
G
H
J
G
H
J
G
H
J
H
J
H
J

V.20

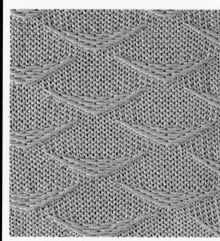

V.18

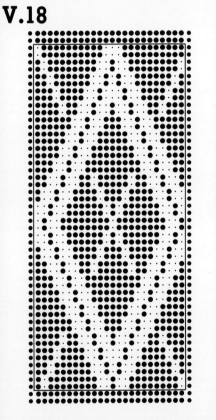

V.19

H
J
H
J

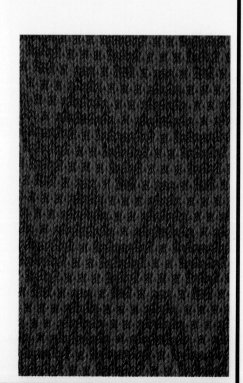

Punchcard instructions and colour key on pages 9 and 10.

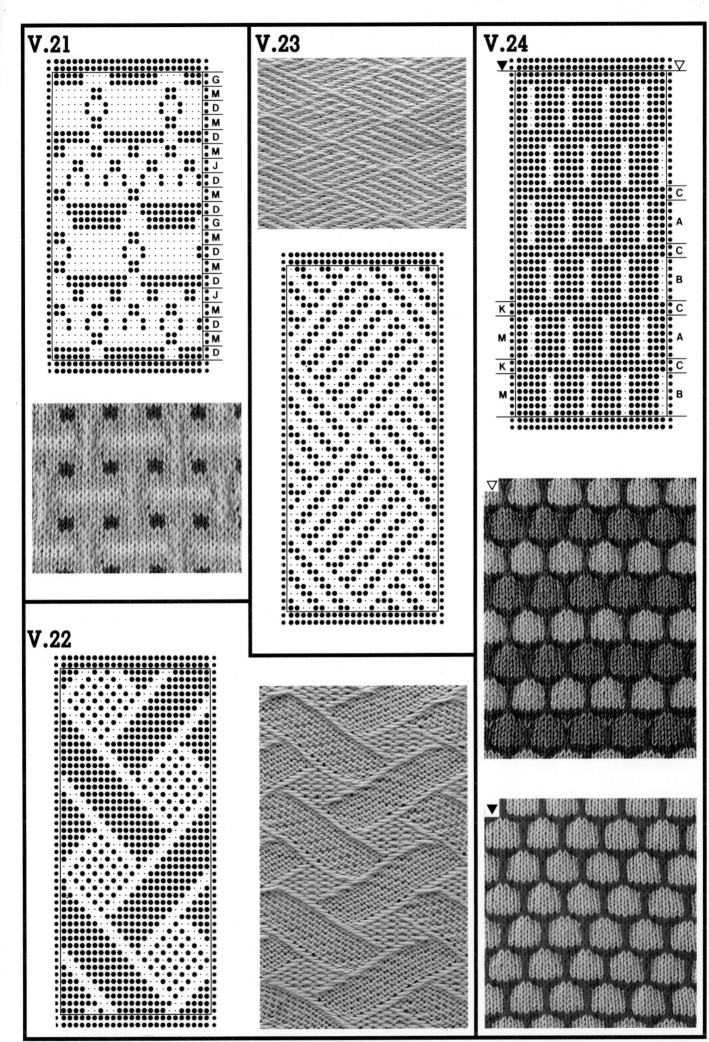

V.21

G
M
D
M
D
M
J
D
M
D
G
M
D
M
D
D
J
M
D
M
D

V.22

V.23

V.24

C
A
C
B
C
A
C
B

K
M
K
M

V. Slip Stitch

V.25

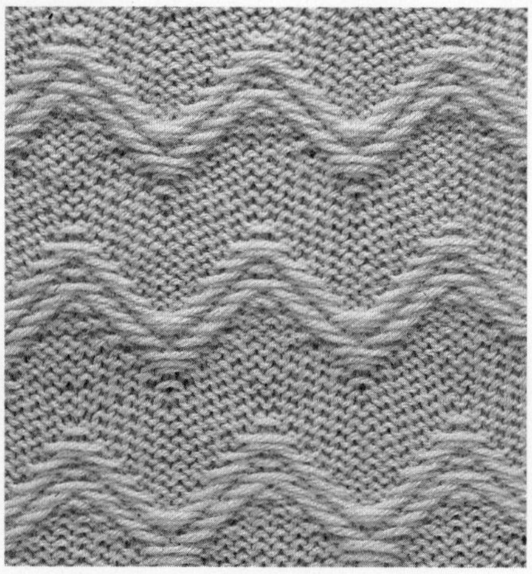

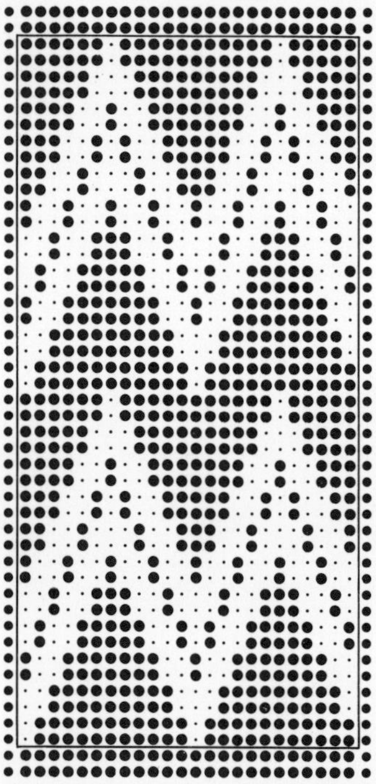

V.27

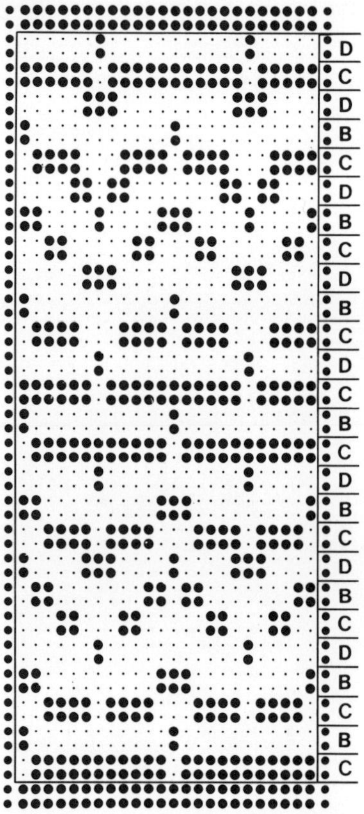

D
C
D
B
C
D
B
C
D
B
C
D
C
B
C
D
B
C
D
B
C
D
B
C
B
C

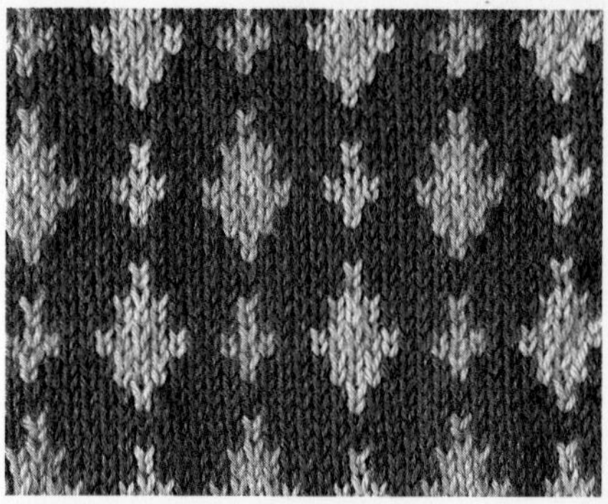

V.28

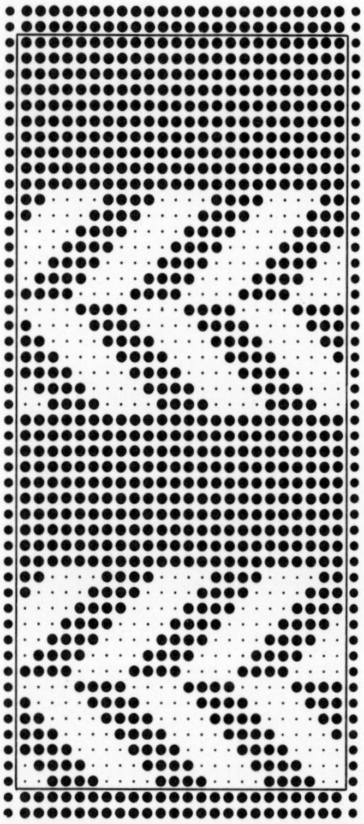

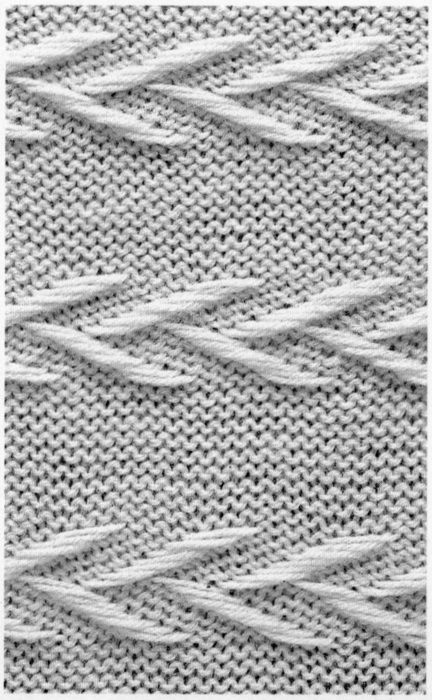

V.26

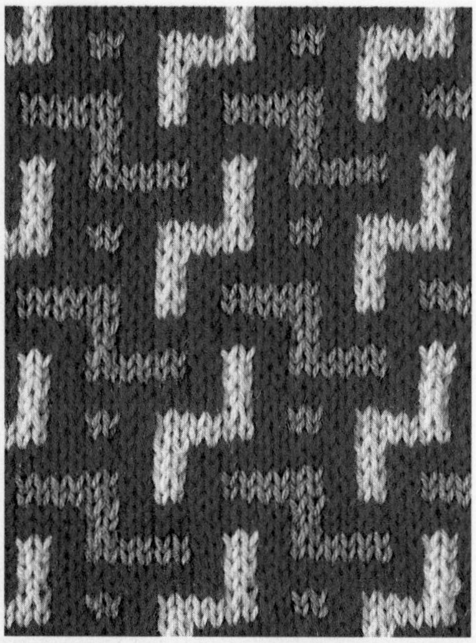

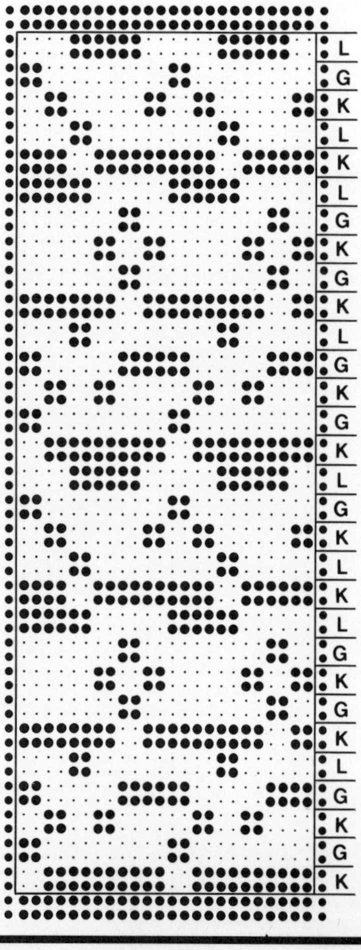

L
G
K
L
K
L
G
K
G
K
L
G
K
G
K
L
G
K
L
K
L
G
K
G
K
L
G
K
G
K

Punchcard instructions and colour key on pages 9 and 10.

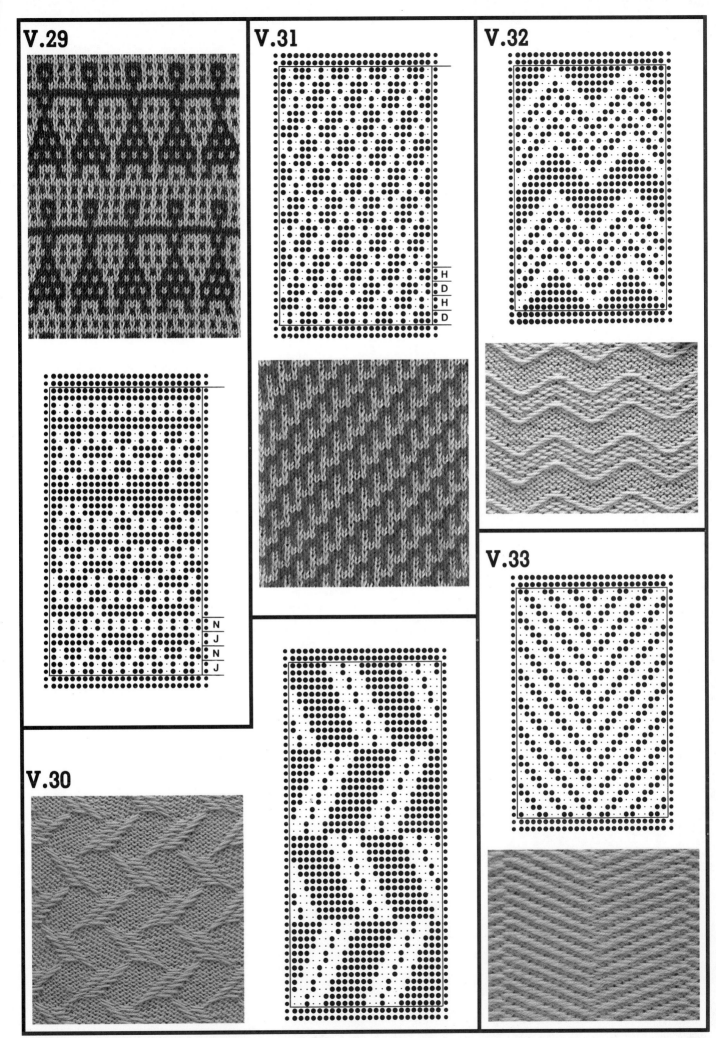

V.29

V.31

V.32

H
D
H
D

N
J
N
J

V.33

V.30

V. Slip Stitch

V.34

V.36

V.38

C
B
F
C
B
F
B
F
C
B
F
C
B
F
B
F

L
M
G
L
M
G

V.35

B
G
B
G
B
G
A
B
G
A
B
G
A
G
A
G
A
G
A
B
G
A
B
G

V.37

Punchcard instructions and colour key on pages 9 and 10.

V.39

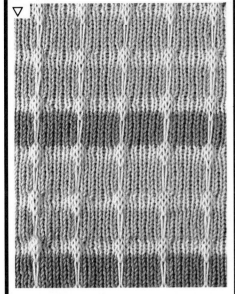

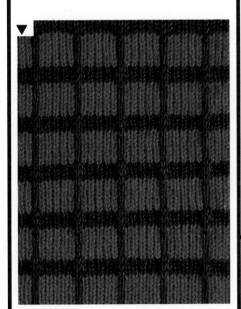

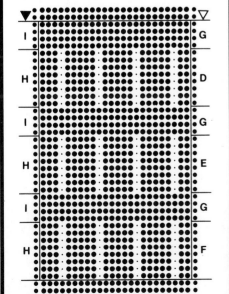

V.40

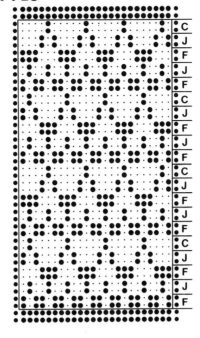

C	
J	
F	
J	
F	
C	
J	
F	
J	
F	
C	
J	
F	
J	
F	
C	
J	
F	
J	
F	

V.41

K	
I	
K	
G	
I	
K	
G	
I	
K	
G	
K	
J	
K	
J	
G	
K	
J	
G	
K	
G	
K	

V.42

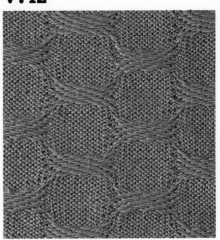

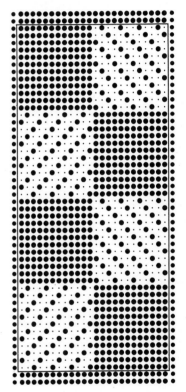

VI. Weaving Patterns

Weaving is plain stocking stitch through which a second thread has been woven under and over the stitches. The needles corresponding to the holes in the punchcard pass the weaving yarn over the stitches formed by the main yarn. The needles corresponding to the blank spaces on the punchcard pass the weaving yarn under the stitches formed by the main yarn.

On non-automatic machines selected needles usually pass the yarn over the stitches formed by the main yarn. Therefore, needles corresponding to the holes in the punchcard should be selected across the entire width of the fabric.

The best weaving fabrics are produced when a fine yarn is used as the main yarn that knits stocking stitch and a thicker or more fancy yarn is used as the weaving yarn. On the diagrams of the punchcards the colour of the 4 ply yarn used for stocking stitch is shown on the left and the colour of the chunky weaving yarn is shown on the right. Even on standard gauge machines it is possible to use a chunky bouclé or hairy yarn to weave with. Try knitting the same punchcard with different weaving yarns to see the variety of effects that can be achieved. Fabrics produced by this method tend to be stable (not stretchy) and are therefore ideal for cut and sew techniques. If a thick yarn is used for weaving it makes good coating or furnishing fabric.

Weaving Patterns with Pick Up

These are produced by knitting the required number of rows as indicated on chart, then using a transfer tool, hooking up indicated weaving threads. The following examples show how this is done.

Weaving Patterns with Pick Up at Back

Worked as Pick Up patterns but hooking up lower weaving threads at the back of the higher ones as indicated in diagram. See VI.34 and VI.42.

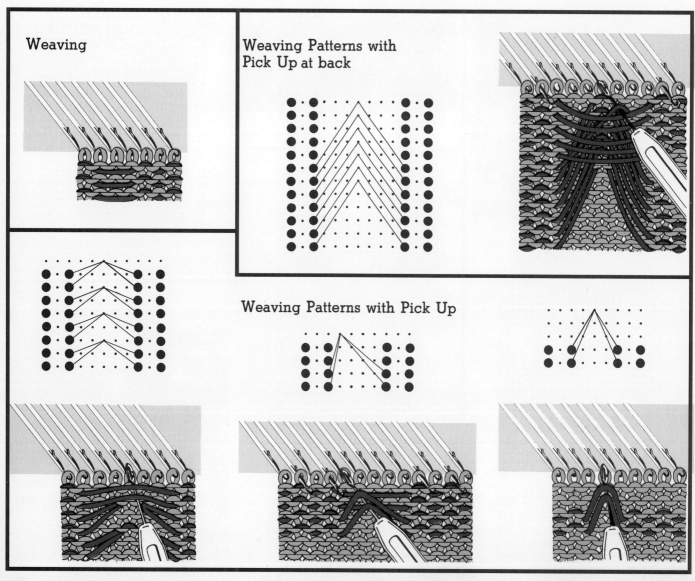

Weaving

Weaving Patterns with Pick Up at back

Weaving Patterns with Pick Up

VI.1

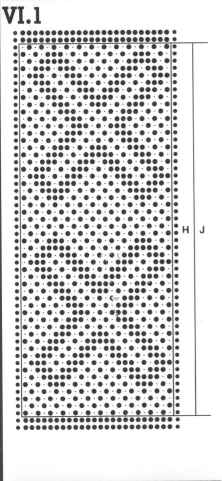

H J

VI.2

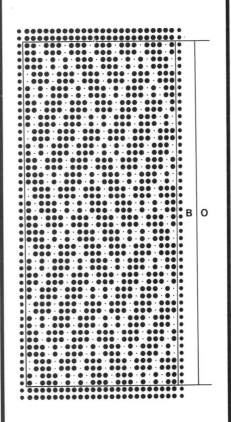

B O

VI.3

VI.4

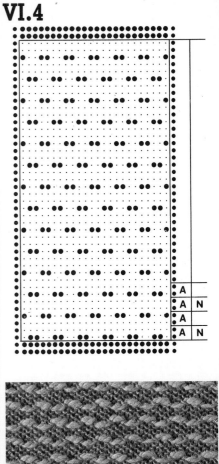

A	
A	N
A	
A	N

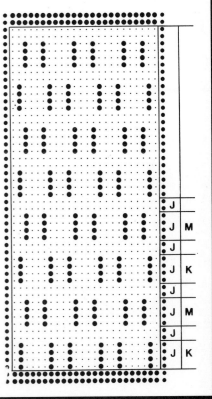

J	
J	M
J	
J	K
J	
J	M
J	
J	K

57

VI. Weaving

VI.5

C G

VI.7

L J

VI.6

VI.8

C
C G
C
C N
C
C D
C
C G
C
C N
C
C D

C
C D
C
C D

L N

Punchcard instructions and colour key on pages 9 and 10.

VI.9

VI.11

VI.12

VI.10

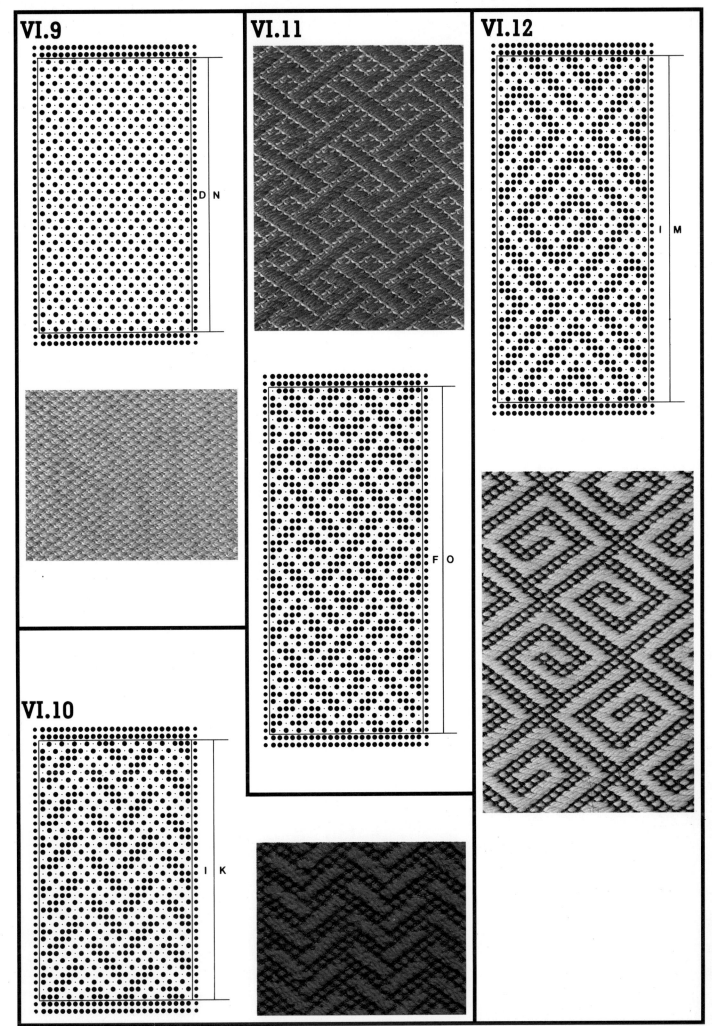

VI. Weaving

VI.13

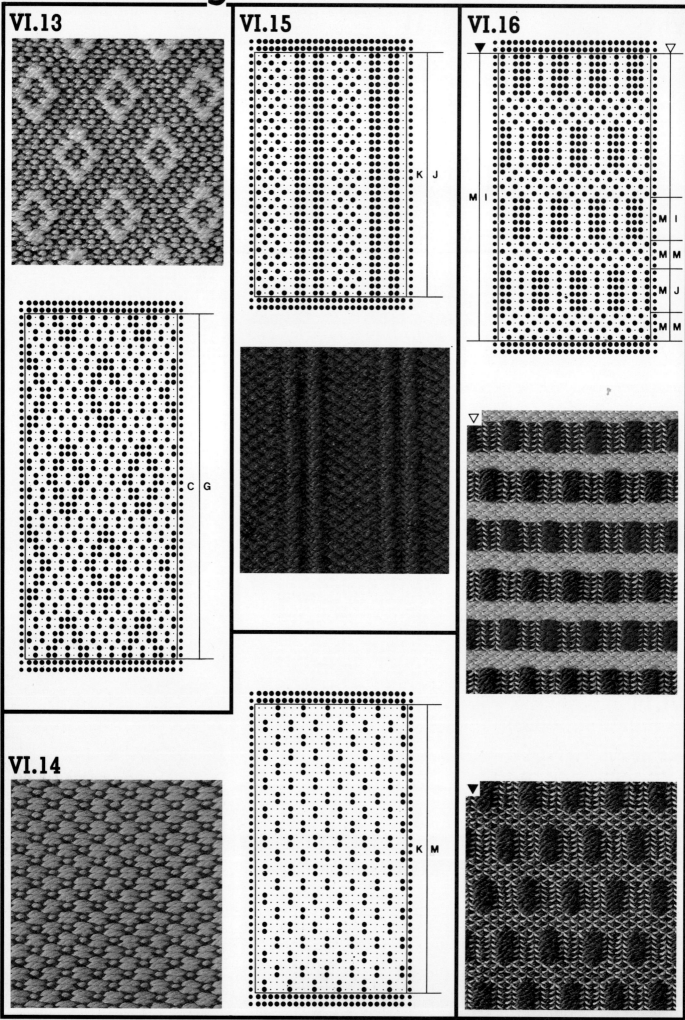

VI.14

VI.15

VI.16

Punchcard instructions and colour key on pages 9 and 10.

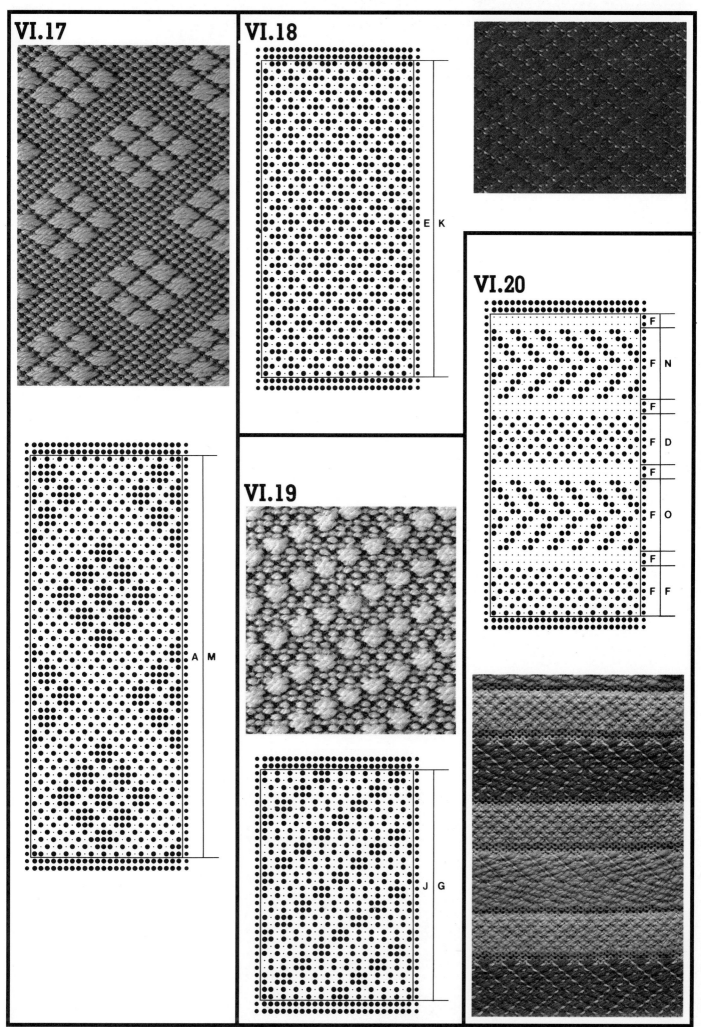

VI.17

VI.18

E K

VI.20

F
F N
F
F D
F
F O
F
F F

A M

VI.19

J G

VI. Weaving

VI.21

G I

VI.22

C G

VI.23

VI.24

I N

L J

Punchcard instructions and colour key on pages 9 and 10.

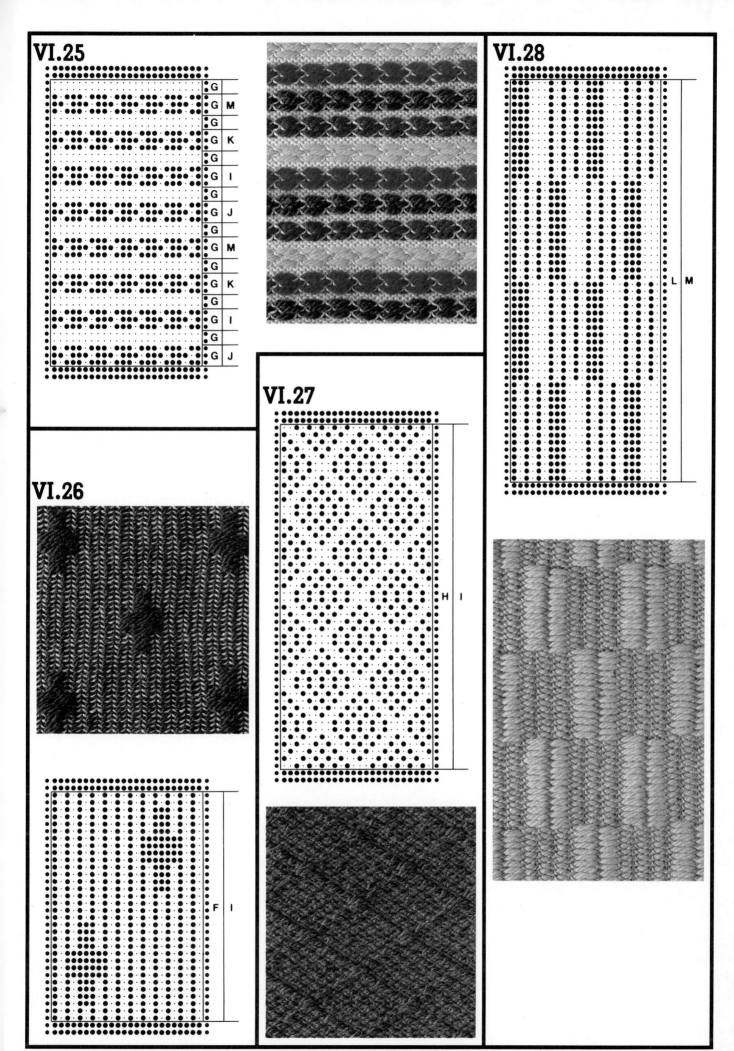

VI.25

	G
	G M
	G
	G K
	G
	G I
	G
	G J
	G M
	G
	G K
	G
	G I
	G
	G J

VI.26

F I

VI.27

H I

VI.28

L M

VI. Weaving

VI.29

VI.31

VI.32

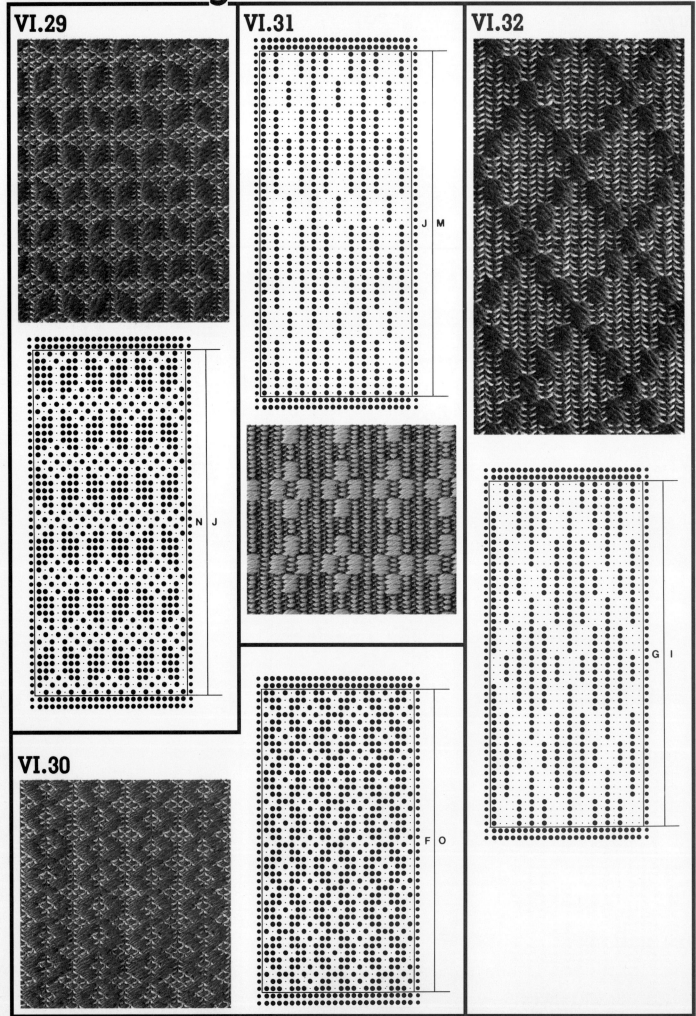

VI.30

Punchcard instructions and colour key on pages 9 and 10.

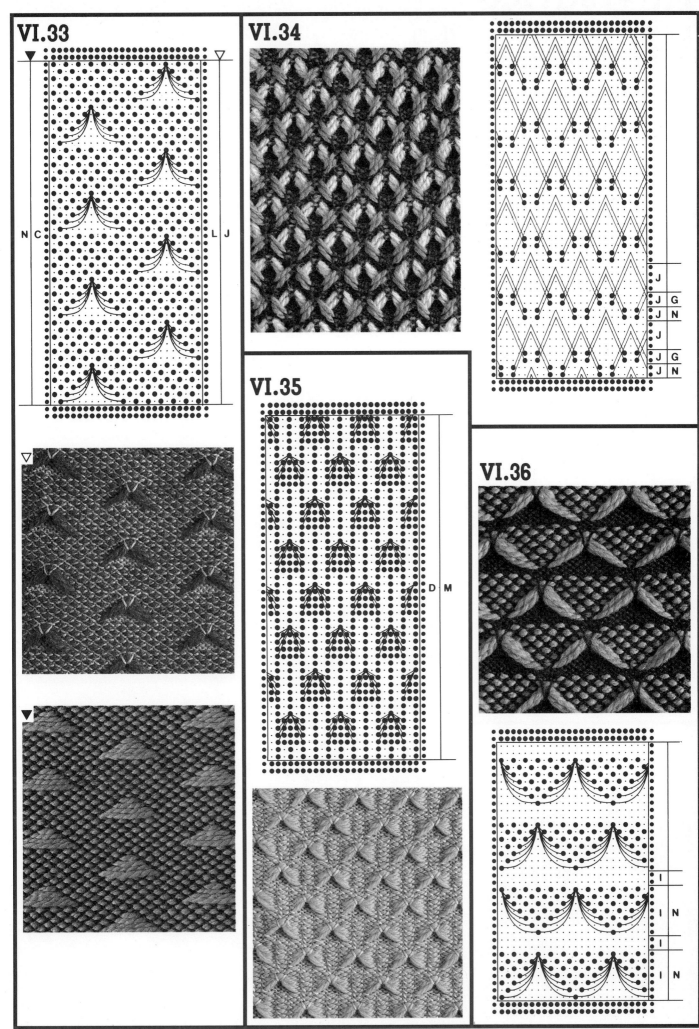

VI.33

N C   L J

VI.34

VI.35

D M

VI.36

J
J   G
J   N
J
J   G
J   N

I
I   N
I
I   N

VI. Weaving

VI.37

VI.38

VI.39

J	
J	G
J	
J	G

F	O
F	M
F	O
F	M

H	
H	J
H	
H	J

VI.40

G O   F O

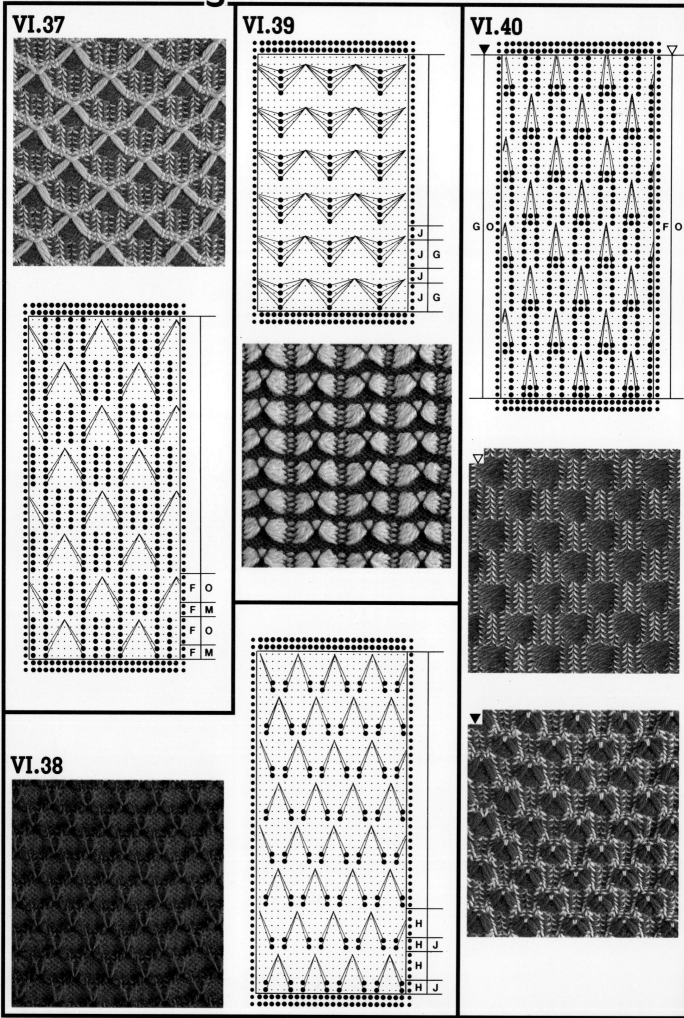

Punchcard instructions and colour key on pages 9 and 10.

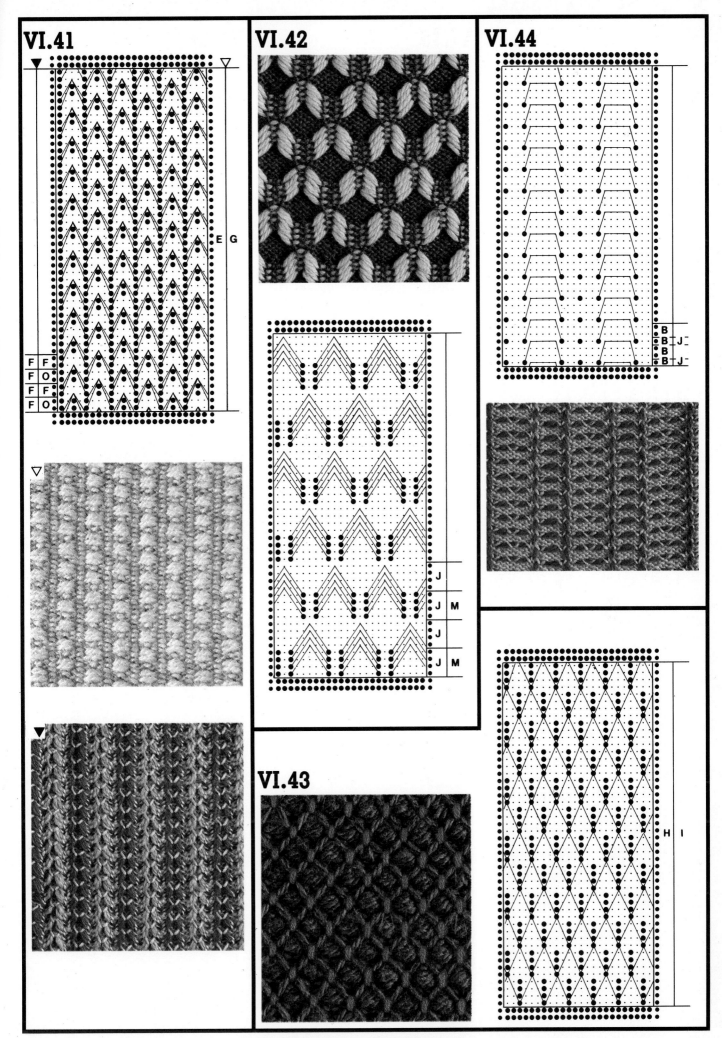

VI.41

E G

F F
F O
F F
F O

VI.42

VI.44

B
B
B
B

J
J

VI.43

J
J
M
J
M

H I

VI. Weaving

VI.45

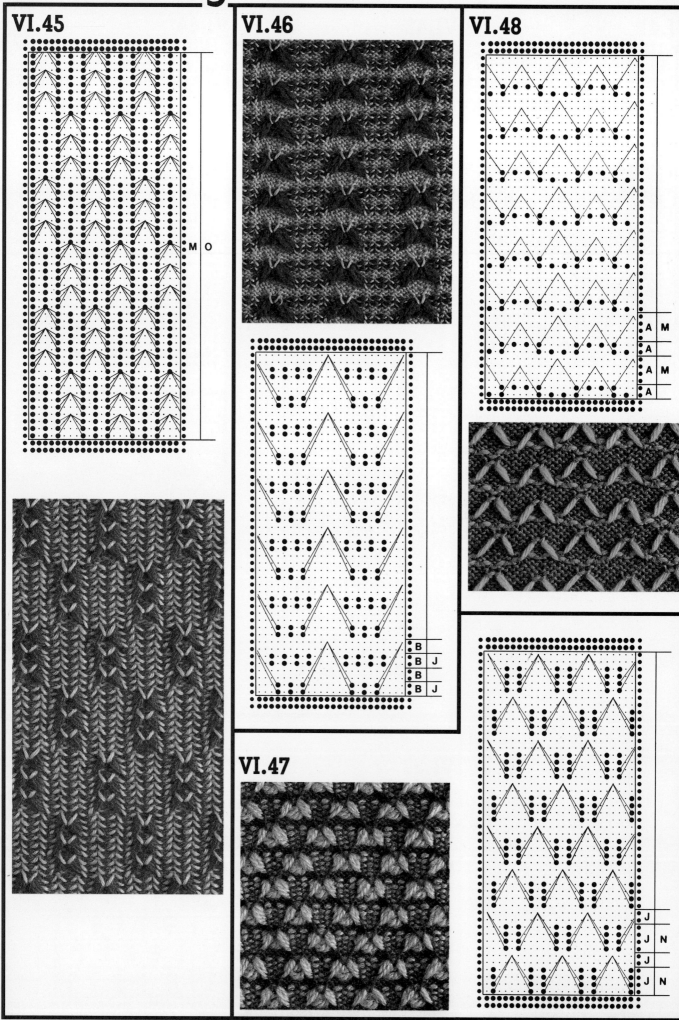

M O

VI.46

VI.47

VI.48

B	
B	J
B	
B	J

A	M
A	
A	M
A	

J	
J	N
J	
J	N

Punchcard instructions and colour key on pages 9 and 10.

These panels and patterns are formed by crossing stitches using latch tools. The following example shows how to cross 3 stitches on right over 3 stitches on left.

To make the cable stand out in stocking stitch one of 3 methods has been used.

1. Leave one needle in Non-Working Position at either side of cable. This method has been used for sample VII.3.

2. As method 1 then using a latch tool knit stitches up to give a purl stitch.

3. Leave two needles in Non-Working Position at either side of cable, then using a latch tool knit stitches up.

It is a good idea to try all three methods before deciding which method is most suitable for a particular piece of work. Methods 2 and 3 have been used for most of the samples in this section.

To make it easier to knit the first row after crossing stitches you may find it helpful to put needles with tight stitches on into Holding Position before knitting the row.

When working all-over patterns, start at the centre and following the guide, transfer all indicated stitches across the entire width of the needles being used before knitting the row.

As these patterns are produced manually they can be worked on non-automatic machines.

Key for Cables and Twists

Cross stitch on left in front of stitch on right.

Cross stitch on right in front of stitch on left.

Cross 2 stitches on left in front of 2 stitches on right.

Cross 2 stitches on right in front of 2 stitches on left.

Cross 2 stitches on left in front of stitch on right.

Cross 2 stitches on right in front of stitch on left.

Cross 3 stitches on left in front of 3 stitches on right.

Cross 3 stitches on right in front of 3 stitches on left.

Cross 3 stitches on left in front of stitch on right.

Cross 3 stitches on right in front of stitch on left.

Cross 3 stitches on right in front of 3 stitches on left, missing stitch at centre.

centre

Needle in Non-Working Position.

3 stitches on right crossed over 3 stitches on left

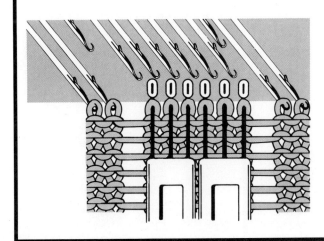
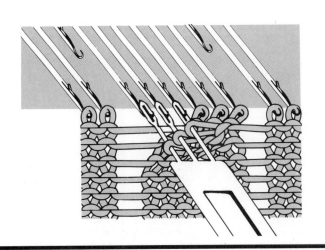

VII. Cable Panels

VII.1

VII.3

VII.5

VII.4

VII.2

VII.6

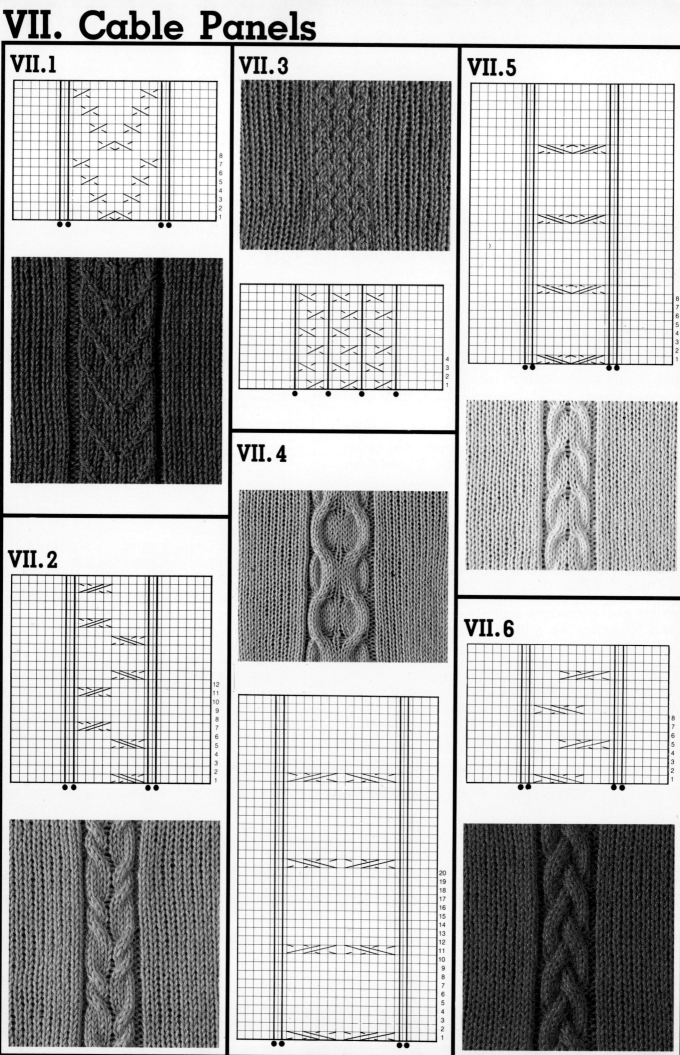

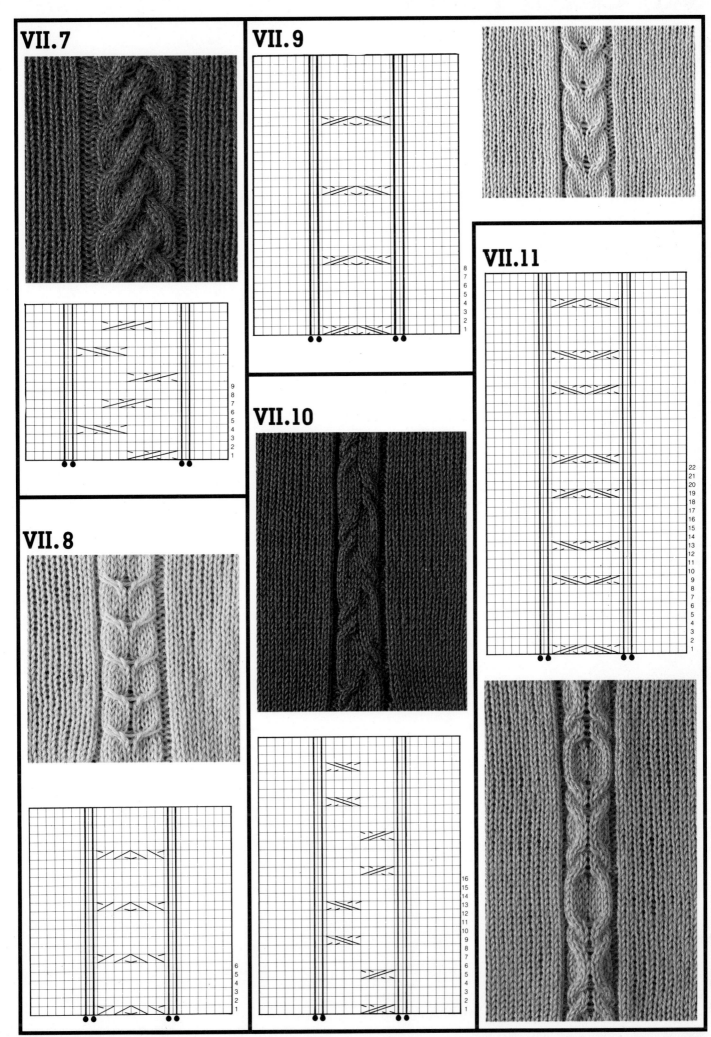

VII.7

VII.8

VII.9

VII.10

VII.11

VII. Cable Panels

VII.12

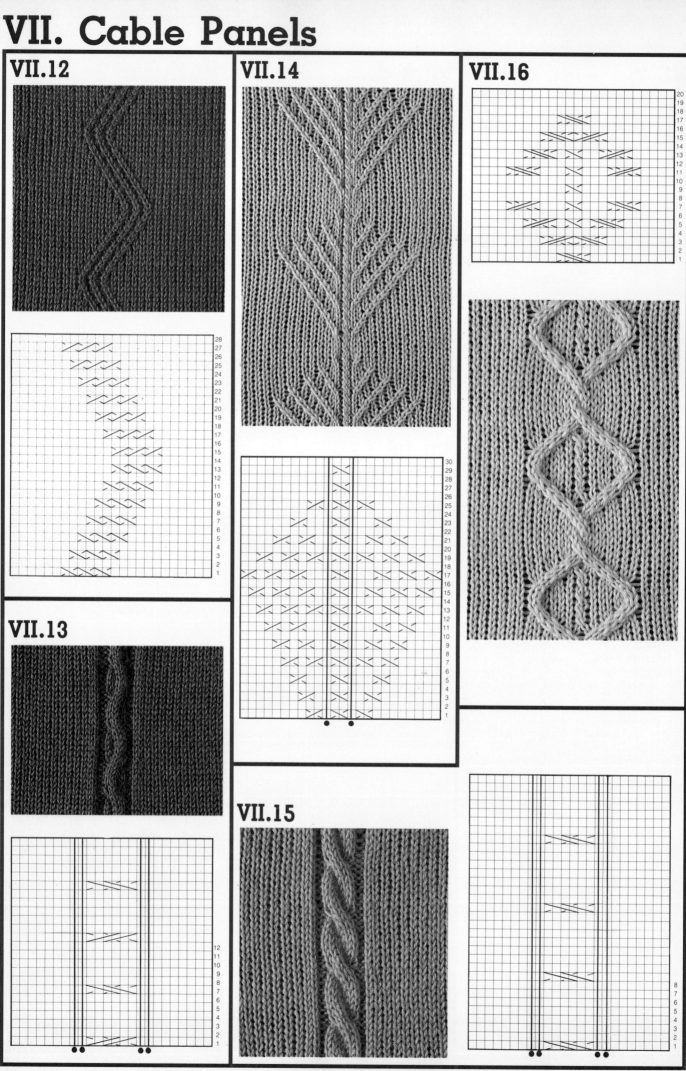

VII.13

VII.14

VII.15

VII.16

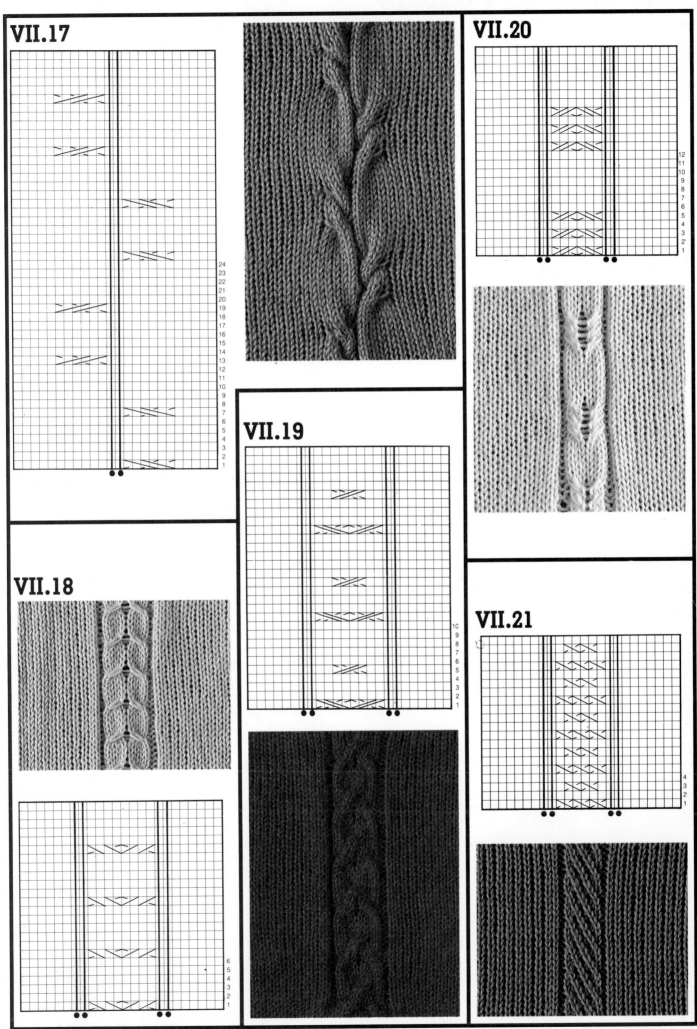

VII.17

VII.18

VII.19

VII.20

VII.21

73

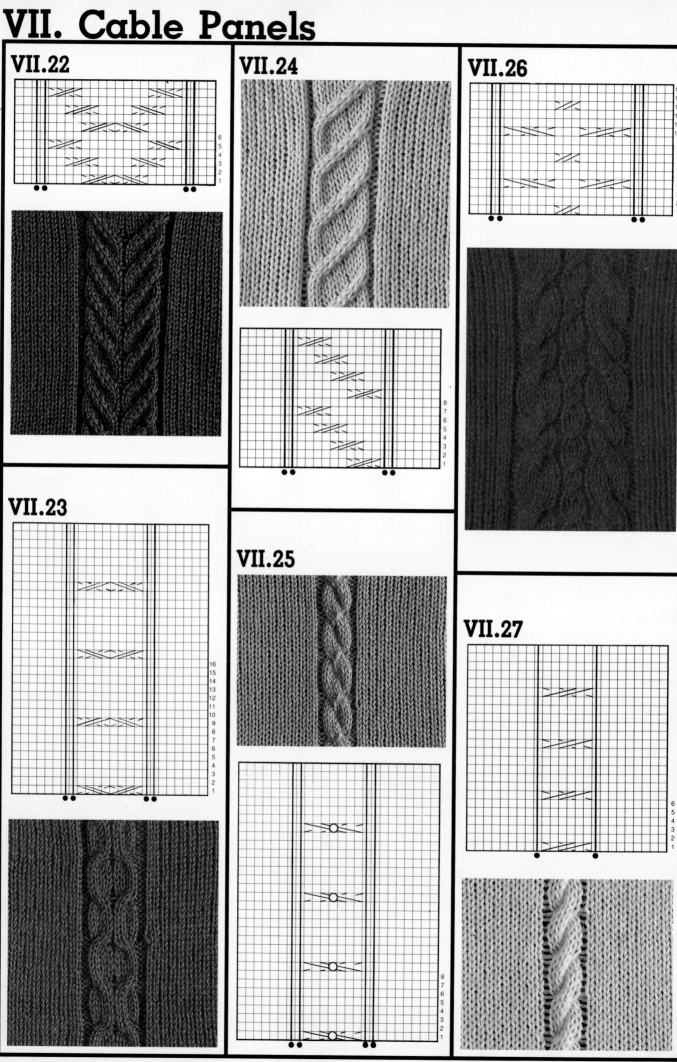

VII.22

VII.24

VII.26

VII.23

VII.25

VII.27

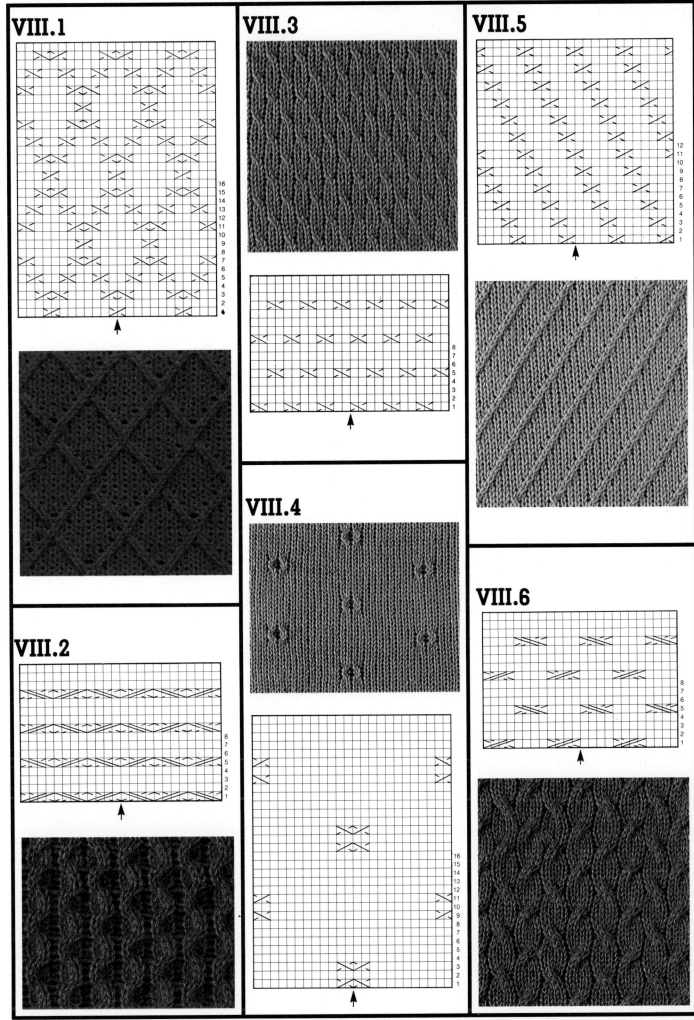

VIII.1

VIII.2

VIII.3

VIII.4

VIII.5

VIII.6

VIII. Cable Patterns

VIII.7

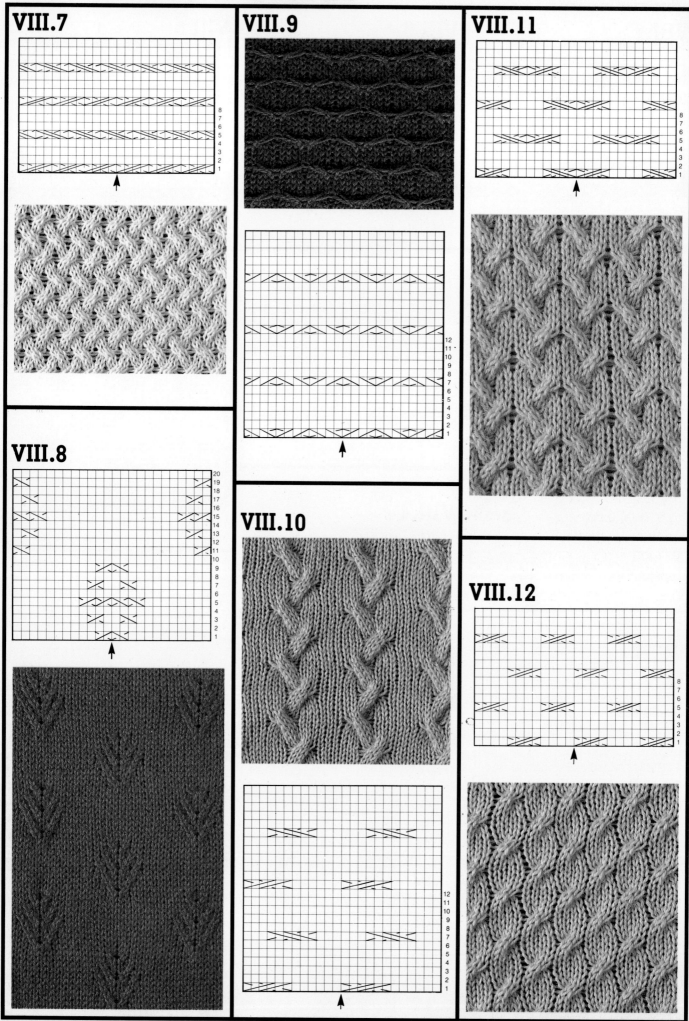

VIII.8

VIII.9

VIII.10

VIII.11

VIII.12

A lace stitch is produced by transferring a stitch onto an adjacent needle. The empty needle remains in Working Position, therefore it continues to knit but it leaves a hole where the stitch has been transferred. Needles corresponding to holes on the punchcard have stitches transferred from them. The direction of the lace carriage determines what needle the stitch is transferred to. For most machines, if the lace carriage is moving from left to right the stitch will be transferred to the needle on the right. If the lace carriage is moving from right to left the stitch will be transferred to the needle on the left. (Some Toyota machines work in a different way therefore owners should consult their manuals). The finished appearance of lace fabric is affected by both the position of the holes and the direction in which the stitches are transferred.

The following example shows one row of lace holes, where every alternate stitch has been transferred to the needle on the left.

To produce lace stitches automatically a lace carriage is required. There are two basic types of lace carriage, one that transfers stitches only and one that transfers stitches and knits. Although either type of lace carriage can knit the punchcards for fancy lace, always use the lace carriage specified with each punchcard.

Lace Carriages that Transfer Stitches and Knit

Machines such as the Knitmaster and some Toyota models (including electronics) have a lace carriage that can knit and transfer stitches on the same row. It is possible to produce lace fabrics on this type of machine with holes on every row.

The following instructions for movement of lace carriage have been used on the punchcard diagrams. They should be copied onto the side of the punchcard and the instructions carried out when they come into view. The instructions refer to the row that is being worked **5 rows below** the row in view. (Some Toyota machines work in a different way therefore owners should consult their manuals).

→ Move lace carriage from left to right.

← Move lace carriage from right to left.

Lace Carriages that Transfer Stitches Only

Machines such as the Jones Brother and some Toyota models (including electronics) have a lace carriage that is used in conjunction with the knit carriage. Lace punchcards for this type of machine are characterised by intervals of unpunched card. These unpunched areas ensure that no needles are selected prior to moving the knit carriage. This can be used as a guide to determine when the knit carriage should be moved. When the lace carriage is on the left-hand side of the needle bed and no needles have been pushed

Production of Lace Fabric

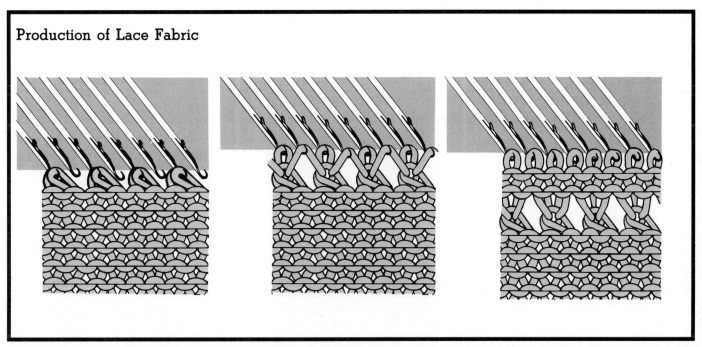

Lace

forward for patterning the knit carriage should be operated.

The following instructions for movement of lace and knit carriage have been used on the punchcard diagrams. They should be copied onto the side of the punchcard and the instructions carried out when they come into view. The instructions refer to the row that is being worked **7 rows below** the row in view. (Some Toyota machines work in a different way therefore owners should consult their manuals).

→ Move lace carriage from left to right.

← Move lace carriage from right to left.

⤵ Knit 2 rows using knit carriage, then move lace carriage in required direction.

4 → Knit 4 rows using knit carriage, then move lace carriage in required direction.

6 → Knit 6 rows using knit carriage, then move lace carriage in required direction.

These instructions can be used to knit fancy lace also.

Fancy Lace

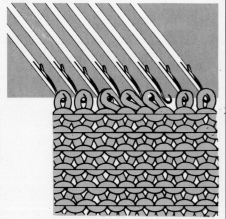

Fancy Lace

Fancy Lace is a term used to describe lace fabrics where stitches are transferred several times in one row. Punchcards are the same for both types of lace carriage, however the following instructions are required for lace carriages that transfer stitches and knit. They should be copied onto the side of the punchcard and the instructions carried out when they come into view. These instructions refer to the row that is being worked **5 rows below** the row in view. (Some Toyota machines work in a different way therefore owners should consult their manuals).

Yarn is out of yarn feeder.
Cam lever set to transfer stitches only.

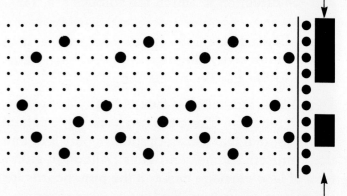

Yarn is in the yarn feeder.
Cam lever set to knit stocking stitch.

IX. Lace (lace carriages that transfer and knit)

IX.1

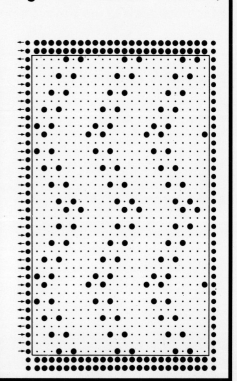

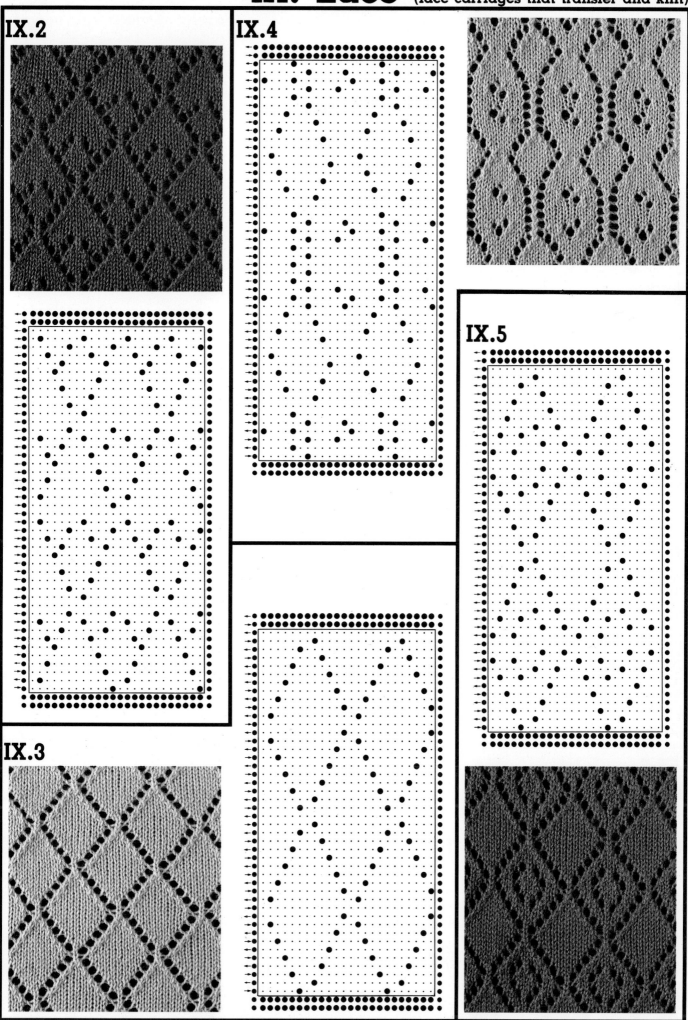

IX.2

IX.4

IX.5

IX.3

IX. Lace (lace carriages that transfer and knit)

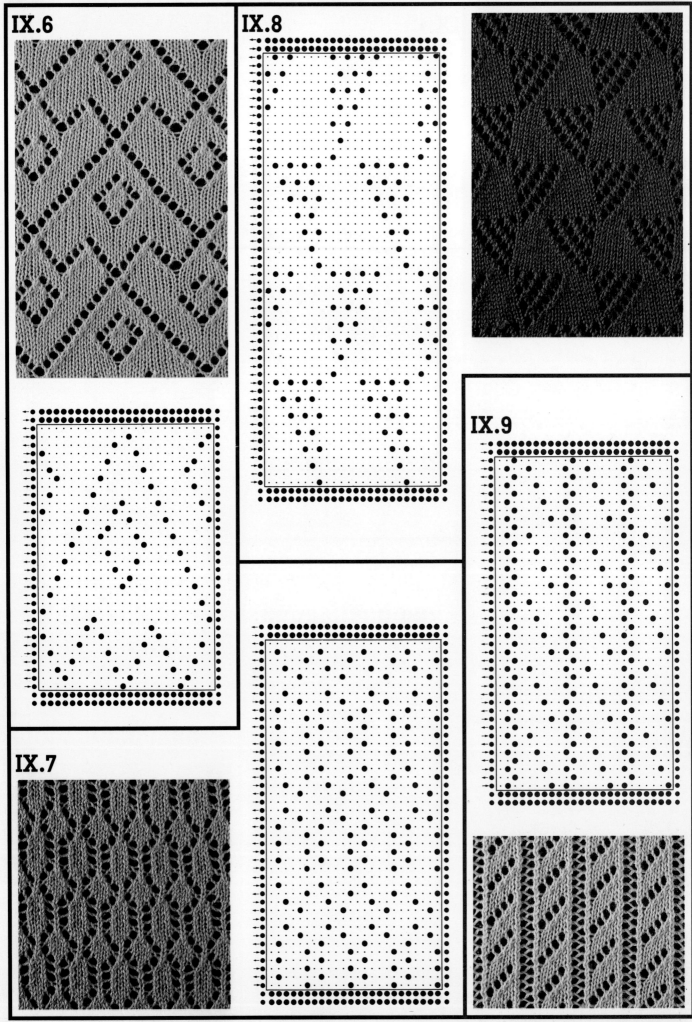

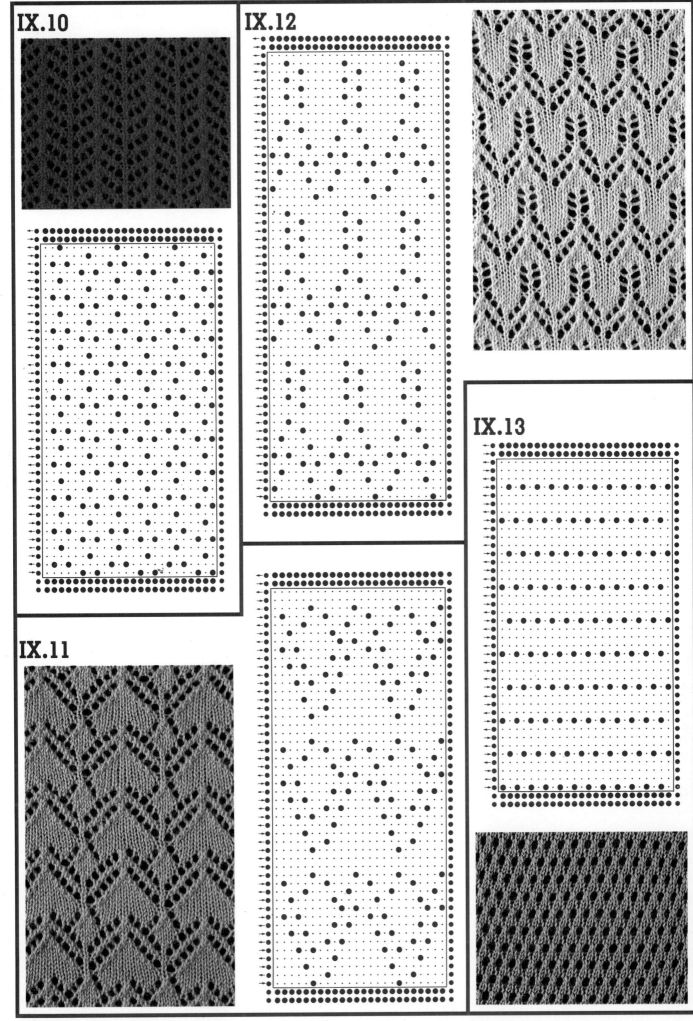

IX.10

IX.12

IX.13

IX.11

IX. Lace (lace carriages that transfer and knit)

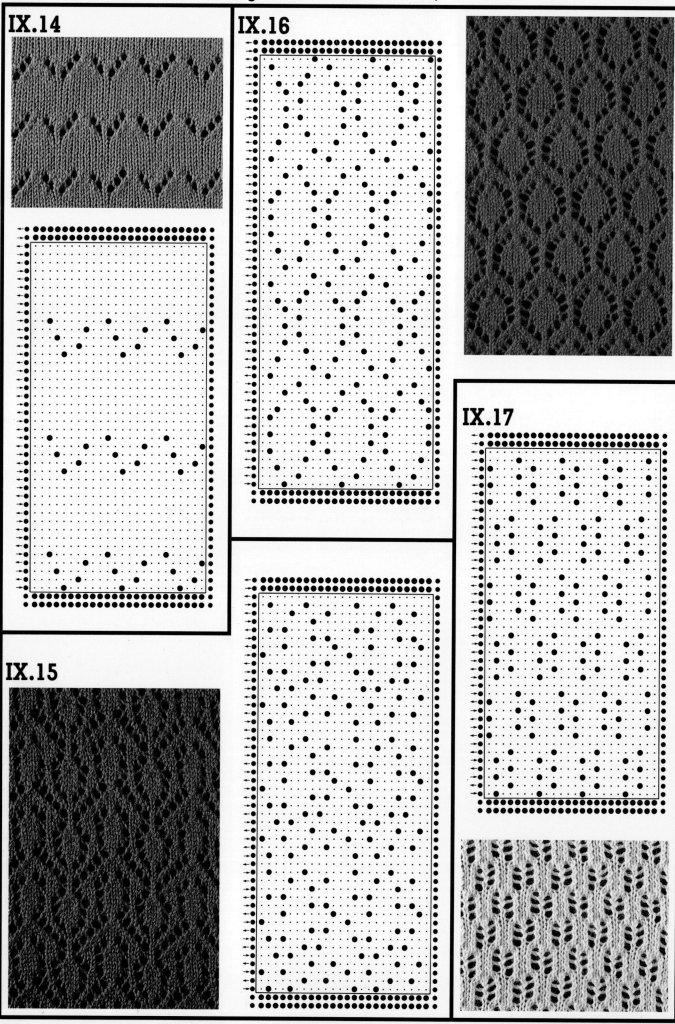

IX.14

IX.15

IX.16

IX.17

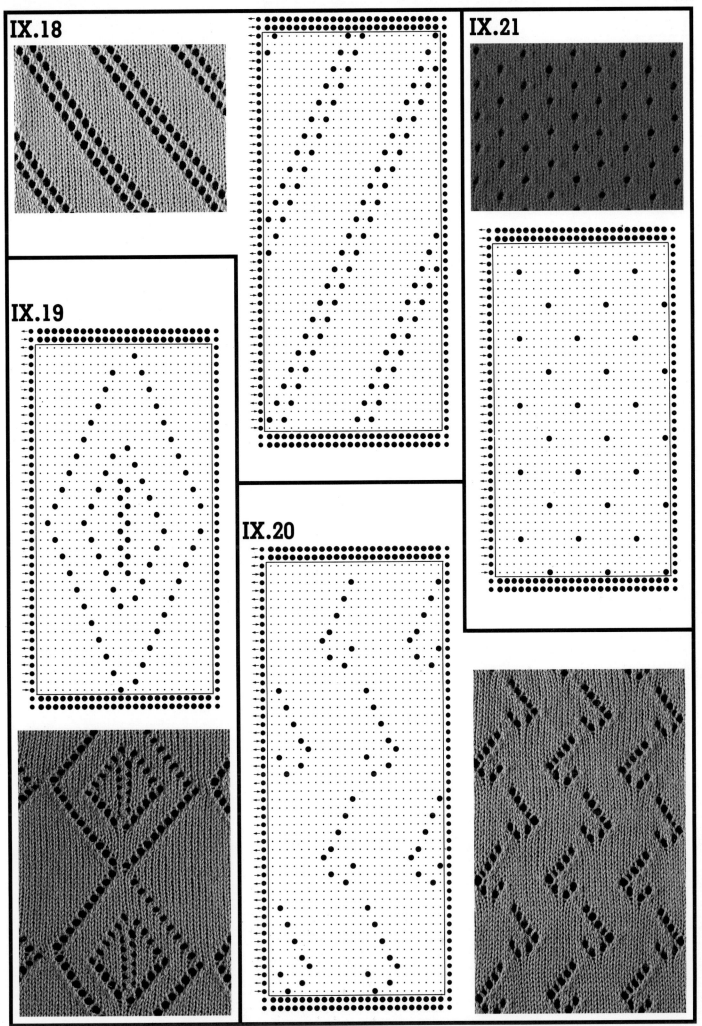

IX.18

IX.19

IX.20

IX.21

IX. Lace (lace carriages that transfer and knit)

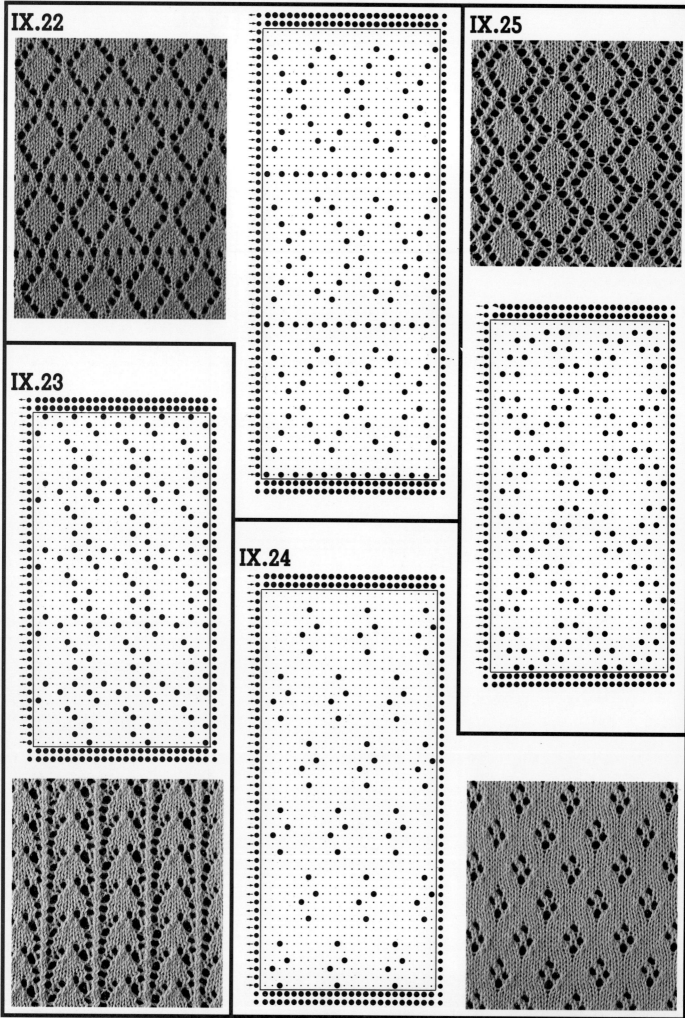

IX.22

IX.23

IX.24

IX.25

IX.25

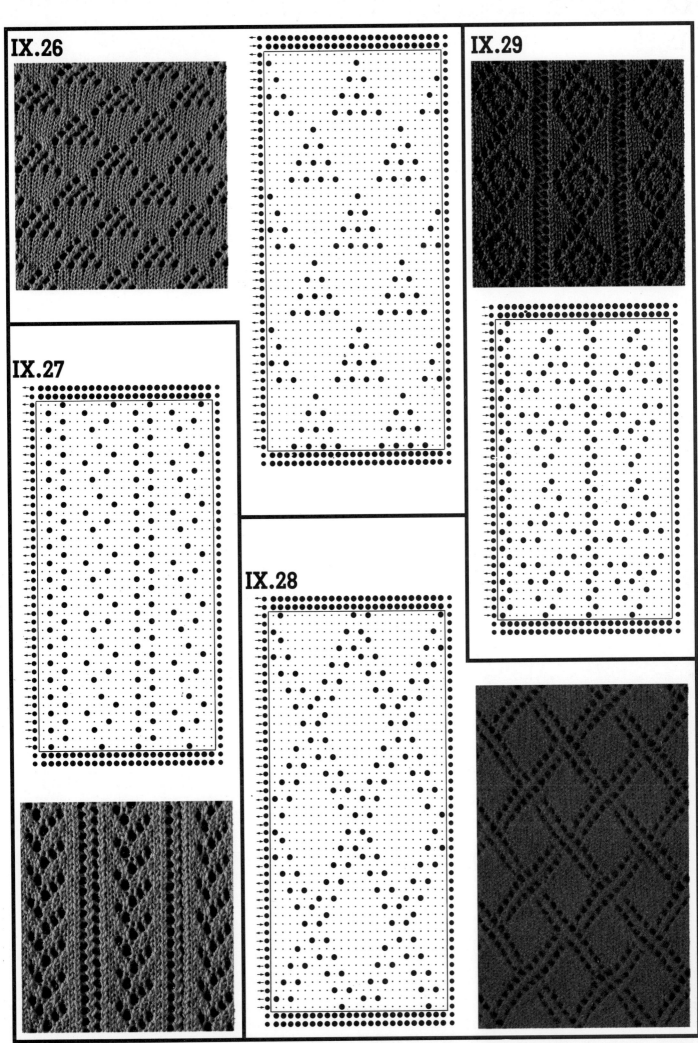

IX.26

IX.29

IX.27

IX.28

IX. Lace (lace carriages that transfer and knit)

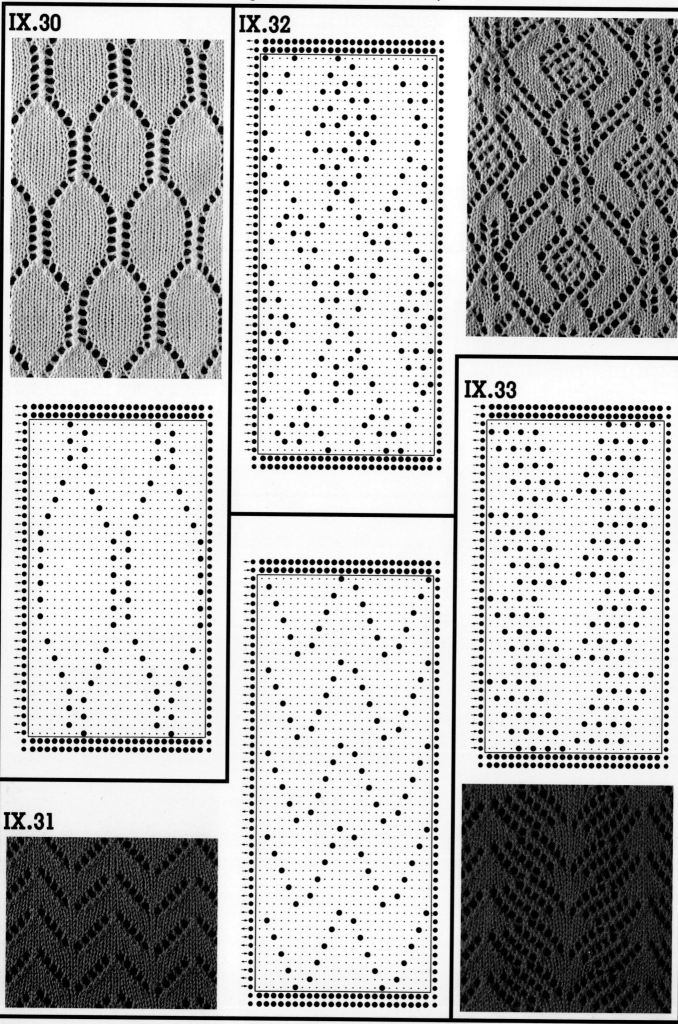

IX.30

IX.31

IX.32

IX.33

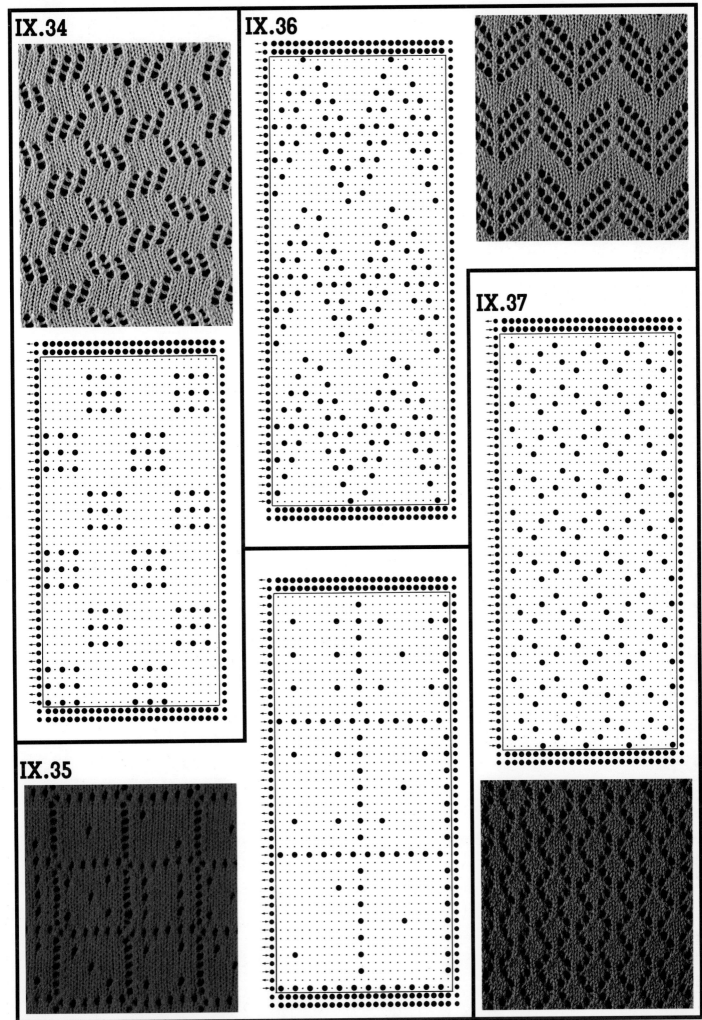

IX.34

IX.36

IX.37

IX.35

X. Lace (lace carriages that transfer only)

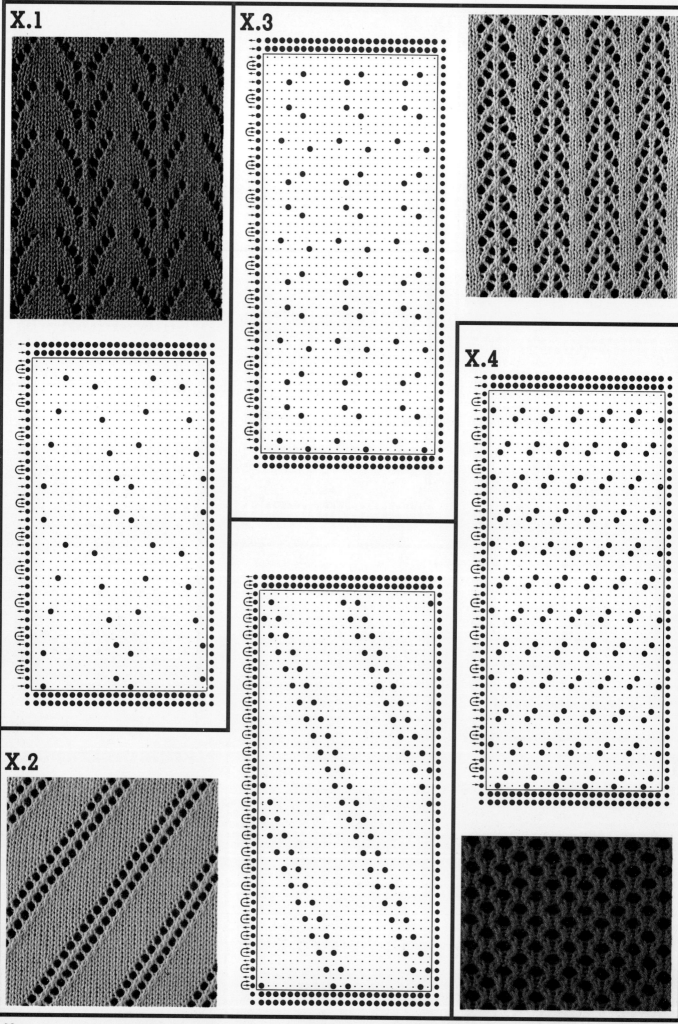

X.1

X.3

X.4

X.2

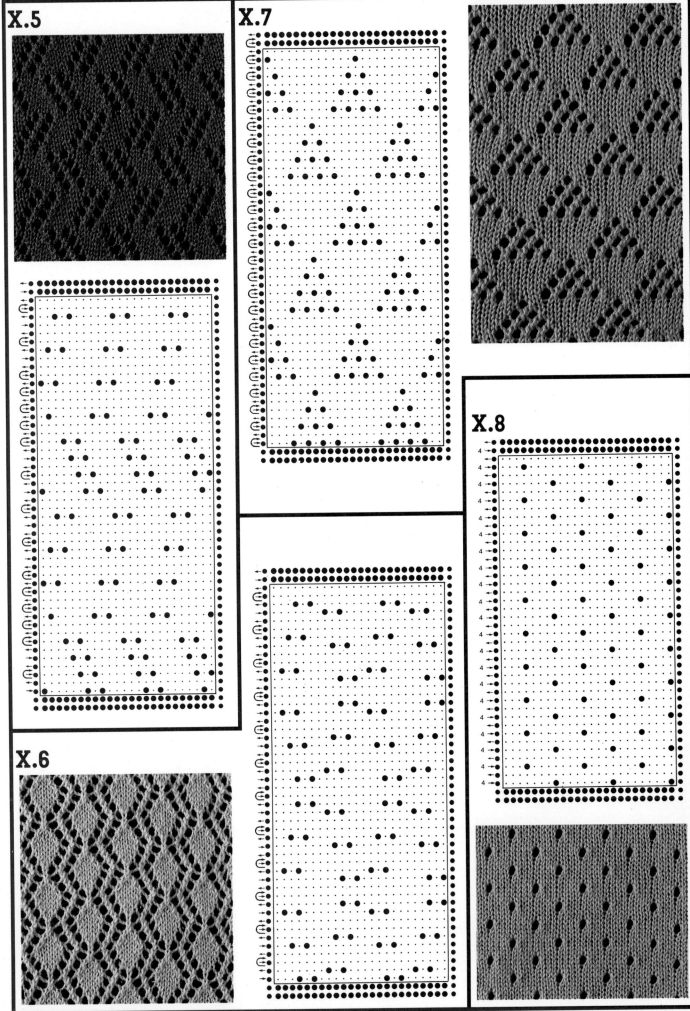

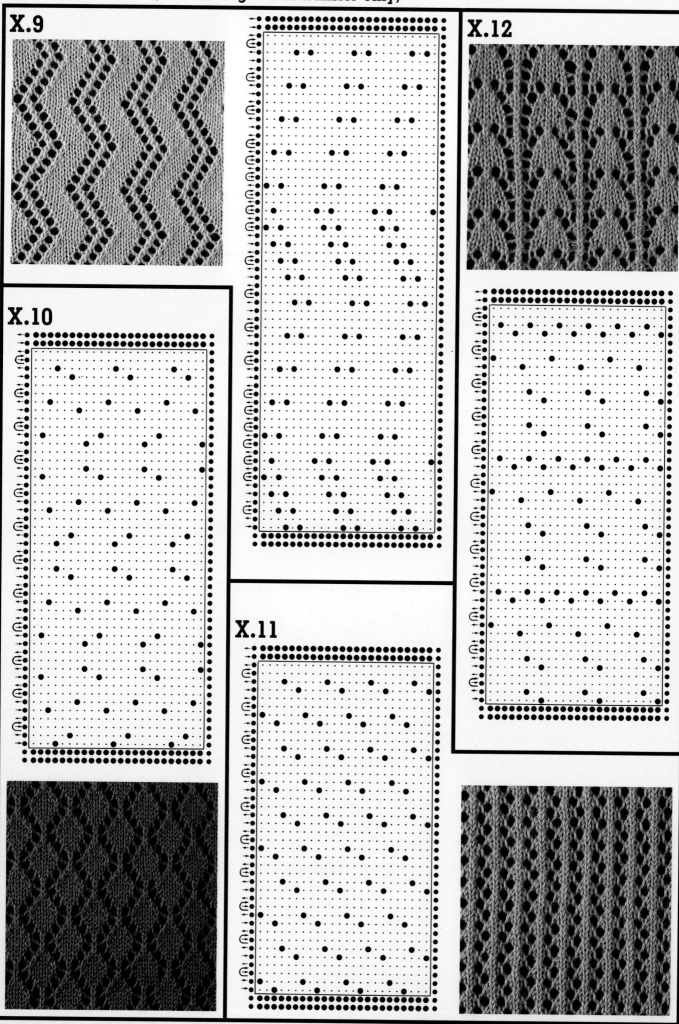

X.9

X.12

X.10

X.11

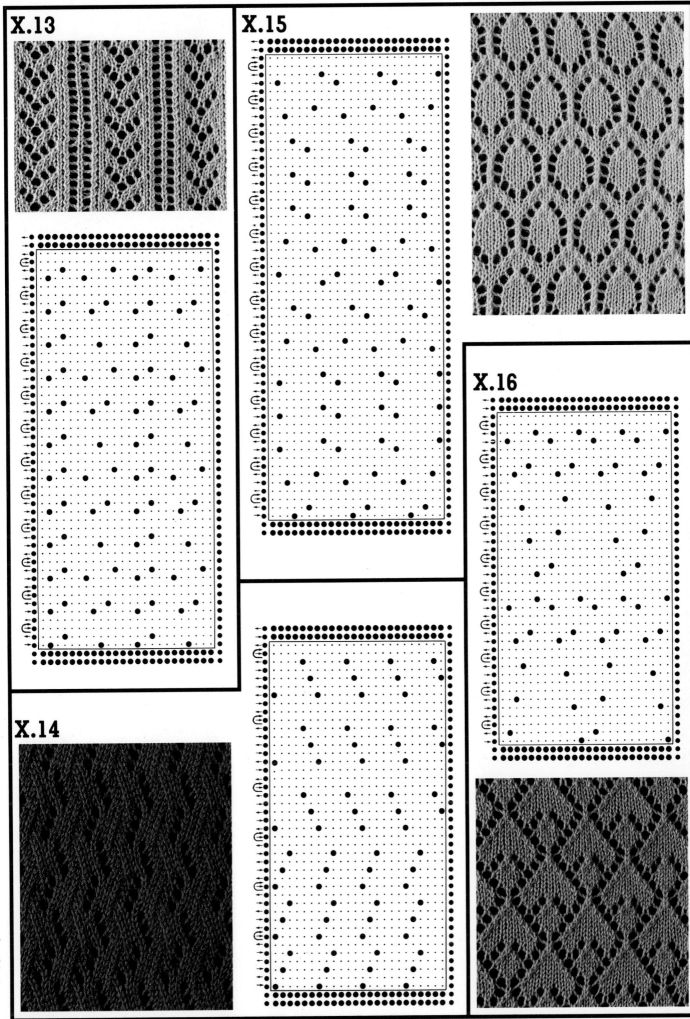

X.13

X.15

X.16

X.14

X. Lace (lace carriages that transfer only)

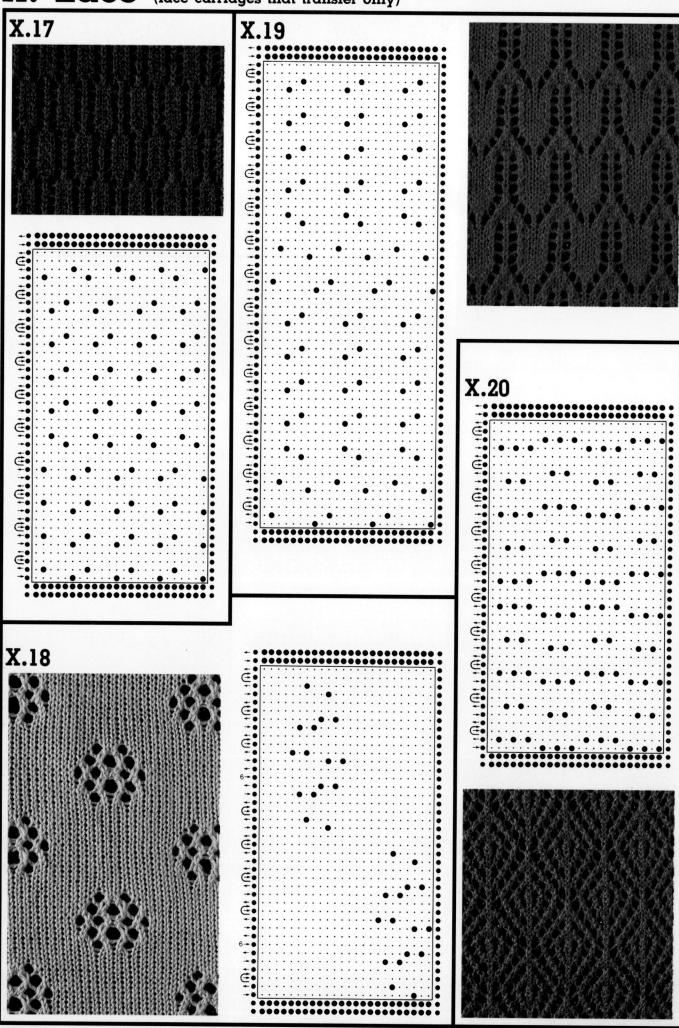

X.17

X.19

X.20

X.18

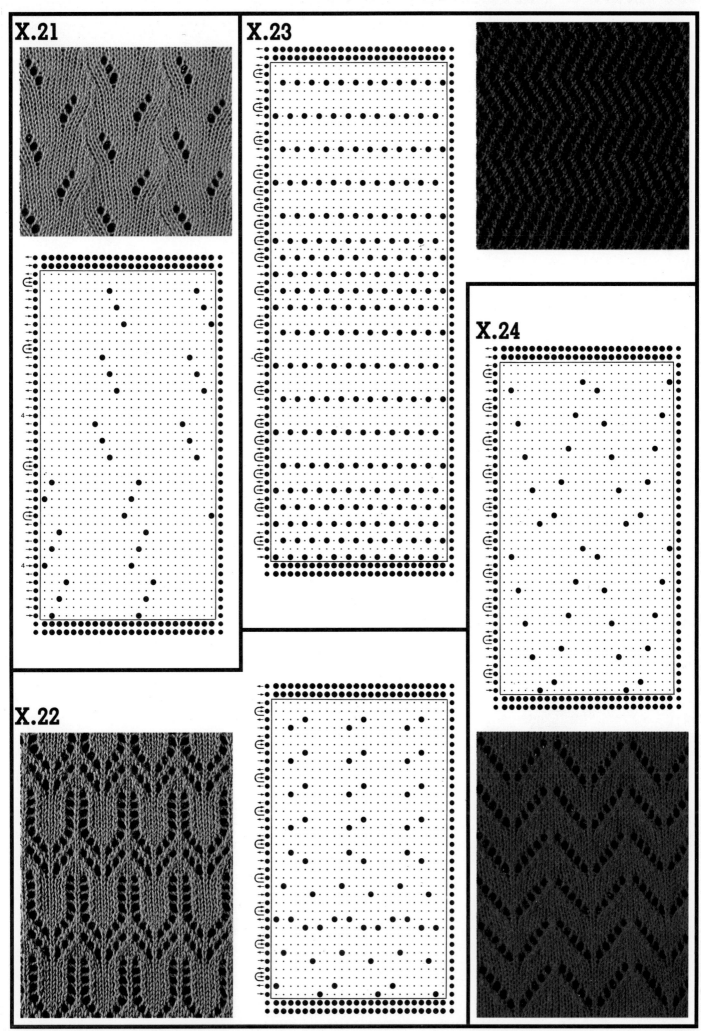

X.21

X.23

X.24

X.22

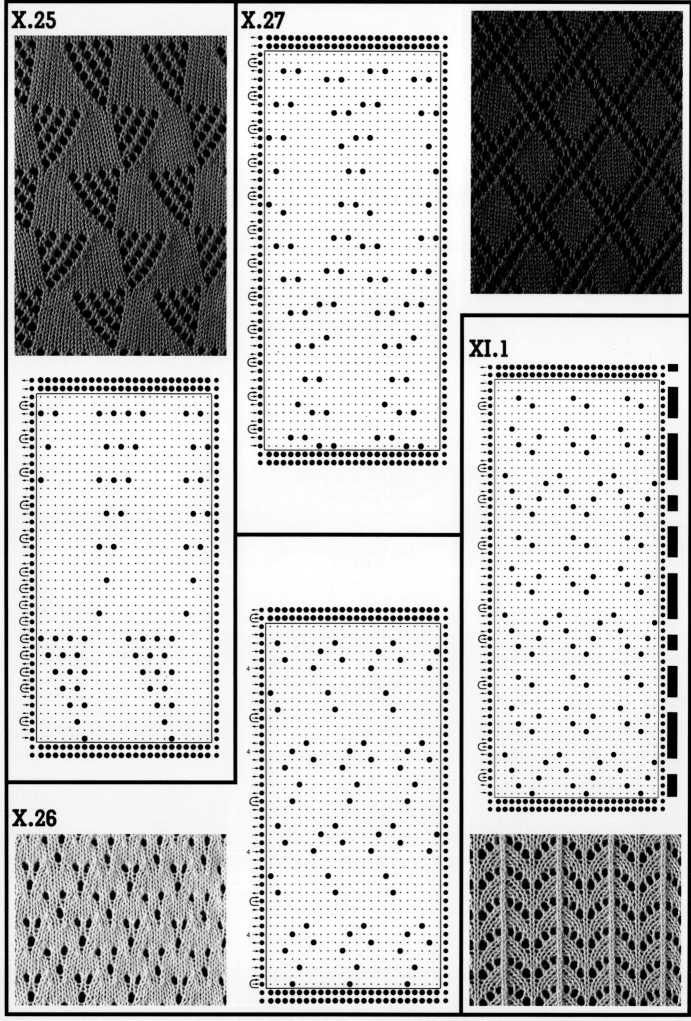

X.25

X.27

XI.1

X.26

XI. Fancy Lace

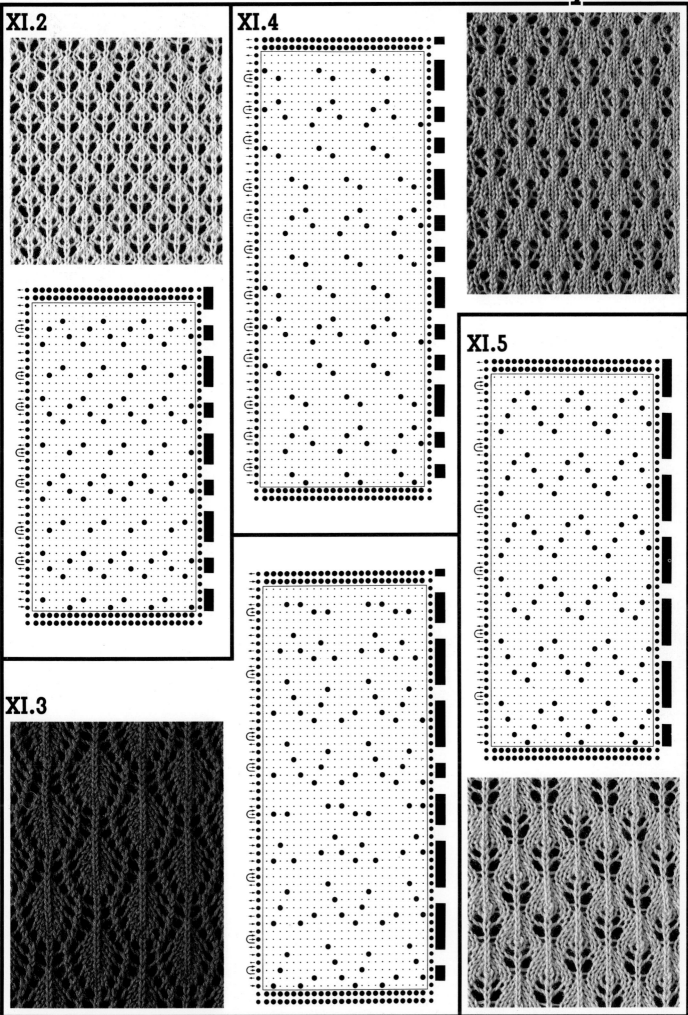

XI.2

XI.4

XI.5

XI.3

XI. Fancy Lace

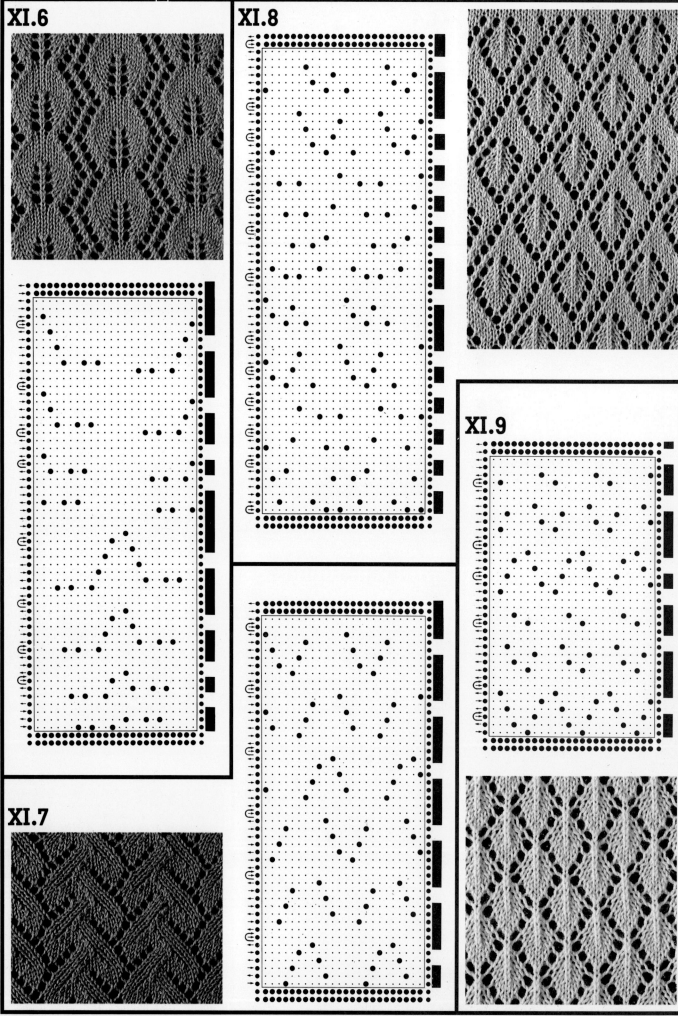

XI.6

XI.8

XI.7

XI.9